800
Ohio State Football
Trivia Q & A

800
Ohio State Football
Trivia Q & A

Mike McGuire

800
Ohio State Football
Trivia Q & A
by Mike McGuire

9780977266128

Published by Mike McGuire

Order copies from
Mike McGuire
27081 N. 96th Way
Scottsdale, AZ 85262
(480) 563-1424

Printed in the United States of America

Dedicated to Buckeye Fans Everywhere

My first book, 500 Ohio State Football Trivia Q & A, *was dedicated to my wife Jackie for her encouragement, support, and suggestions. In the last two years Jackie has become a "True Buckeye Fan" and just loves the "Ramp Entrance" by TBDBITL. Plus she throws one hell of a party when the Buckeyes come to town in Scottsdale, Arizona.*

With this second edition of Ohio State football trivia, I dedicate this book to all the wonderful Buckeye Fans from around the world as sales of the first edition truly went "around the world." Ohio State football is not just a local college sport in Columbus, Ohio or a team from Ohio, but Ohio State football has a global following. I greatly appreciate all the support and the wonderful comments I have received from Buckeye fans about the first edition. This has driven me to improve and add a few new features, expand, and update the trivia questions. My hope is that you will enjoy 800 Ohio State Football Trivia Q & A *more than the first edition of 500 trivia questions, and that you always keep your eye on the prize...BEAT MICHIGAN.*

Introduction

The Ohio State University football program has more great traditions, along with historical games and noteworthy players than any other college football program in the United States. *800 Ohio State Football Trivia Q & A* covers all these great traditions, happenings, and events of Buckeye Football including, but not limited to, The Band, The Teams, The Award Winners, Buckeye Leafs, The Players, Brutus Buckeye, Block "O," The "Horseshoe," Script Ohio, and the greatest rivalry in all of college football, "The Game," with the University of Michigan Wolverines. Coaches Wilce, Schmidt, Brown, Fesler, Hayes, Bruce, Cooper, Tressel, and others, all have their own Trivia Q & A.

The purpose of writing this book on Ohio State Football Trivia was one of just plain fun. To enhance the reader's knowledge of the "Battling Buckeyes" and to increase one's overall enjoyment of the "History and Traditions of Ohio State Football" was just an additional benefit.

Mike McGuire
Go Bucks!™ **BEAT MICHIGAN.**

Ohio State Football Trivia

In retirement, I am writing a series of trivia books; you just can't play golf and gin everyday. The *800 Ohio State Football Trivia Q & A* book is my third trivia book and uses the same format of 20 questions and 20 answers per group.

The Ohio State football trivia questions are meant to be fun, thought-provoking, and bring back good ole' memories of what it means to be a "True Buckeye Fan." Laugh, cry, argue—but have fun with the trivia!

Many of the questions/answers come from "off the top of my head," from the many years in the "Shoe," and the many hours arguing and discussing Ohio State football in local pubs and pizza joints. I used the internet and several books (see bibliography section) to verify a lot of the questions/answers and for ideas and directions for you to ask and answer the trivia. I strongly recommend collecting and reading the books in the Ohio State Football Bibliography at the end of this book. There are 10 new books in just the last two years on Ohio State football!

How to Use
800 Ohio State Football Trivia Q & A

Trivia questions are always meant to be fun, tricky, thought-provoking and confusing, while testing one's knowledge of a particular subject. *800 Ohio State Football Trivia Q & A* is no different. We do offer the following suggestions on "How to Use" the Ohio State Football Trivia Q & A book for greater enjoyment.

It is great to use as a "party starter" for any Buckeye gathering before kick-off and an excellent way to meet new people while also learning about the great traditions of Ohio State football. The book is laid out in a format of 20 questions and answers and Buckeye fans can go along at their own pace. Each correct answer could be worth 5 points within a group of questions, and individuals or teams awarded prizes for their skill and knowledge of Ohio State football trivia.

Tail-Gating...A great way to pass the time as the hamburgers and hotdogs are cooking on the grill. Play to see who cooks or who cleans up after the meal!

On-the-Road...Driving to and from an Ohio State game, trivia can help make the miles pass faster. Play to see who drives and who asks the questions, or who buys the next tank of gas, food, or cocktails.

On-an-Airplane...A great way to study and improve your knowledge of Ohio State football. Upon your arrival impress your Ohio State friends with your trivia knowledge of Ohio State football. Maybe even meet other Ohio State fans on the plane.

Local Pub or Pizza Joint...A pizza and beer always taste better with great sports trivia conversations, discussions and arguments, and it doesn't get any better than Ohio State football.

First-Date at OSU...Not recommended unless there is prior knowledge of the other person's love for Ohio State football.

On-a-Bus or train...see airplane above.

In-the-bathroom...OK!, but please keep the book on your night stand or a bookshelf.

Send me the unique ways you have used the *800 Ohio State Football Trivia Q & A* book.

Go Bucks!™ BEAT MICHIGAN.

Author Mike McGuire's Buckeye Bio

I have been fortunate to be part of four generations of McGuire's whose blood runs Scarlet and Gray. My Grandfather McGuire watched "Chic" Harley play at The Ohio Field, donated to the construction of the Ohio Stadium and had B-box seats for nearly six decades. My other grandfather Reiter was the first in the family to graduate from Ohio State with a degree in Veterinary Medicine shortly after World War I. My mom graduated in 1938, my dad was a football manager for Francis Schmidt and later for many years was an usher on the track until the late 1970s. My brother Terry graduated from Ohio State in 1965 and may be crazier than I am about Ohio State football. My daughter is the one who sits in the "Horseshoe" and holds up the sign "DAD, SEND MORE MONEY!" My son may be more of a football nut than my brother.

I started to go to the "Horseshoe" at the age of seven in 1954 and was indoctrinated into becoming a "Buckeye Fan" with the likes of "Hopalong" Cassady, Hubert Bobo, Dave Leggett and Jim Parker. I never missed a home game from 1954 until I went to Vietnam in 1967, but I returned in time to go to the 1969 Rose Bowl and see the National Champion Buckeyes beat O.J. Simpson and the Southern Cal Trojans.

Returning to Ohio State as a student, I took Woody's course on Coaching Football as an elective. It was a great course because Coach Hayes was far and above the best professor "teacher" I had at Ohio State, and I had many noteworthy professors. I continued my string of home games from 1969 until retiring in Arizona in 2004. With a great Buckeye fan base and Alumni Club here in Scottsdale, Arizona, every game is on TV at a local sports bar so I keep in touch every Saturday in the Fall with the "Battling Buckeyes."

Over the years I've been to nearly 300 games in the Ohio Stadium and dozens more at other schools, Big Ten Schools and Bowl Games. I look forward to continuing as a Buckeye Fan and my grandchildren becoming the fifth generation of McGuires whose blood runs Scarlet and Gray.

TABLE OF CONTENTS

QUESTIONS GROUP 1

1-1 What is the proper name of "The Horseshoe," Home of The Ohio State University Buckeyes?

1-2 What is the official Ohio State University Mascot?

1-3 Head Coach Woody Hayes coached from what season to what season?

1-4 **T or F** The OSU Faculty Council voted against the 1961 Big Ten Champions going to the Rose Bowl.

1-5 What year was Head Coach Earle Bruce inducted into the College Football Hall of Fame?

1-6 Ohio State and Michigan have met continuously since what year?

1-7 What was "The 10 Year War?"

1-8 What is the Ohio State student body cheering section called?

1-9 What is Athlon Sports No. 1 greatest college football tradition?

1-10 What game called "The Upset of the Century" was Ohio State's most costly defeat?

1-11 Who won the Outland Trophy and Lombardi Award in 1970 and is a member of the College Football Hall of Fame?

1-12 Where is the "Victory Bell" located?

1-13 Total attendance in "The Shoe" since 1922 is approximately how many million fans?

1-14 Which fullback delivered the best on Woody Hayes' philosophy "Three Yards and a Cloud of Dust?"

1-15 Name the three Ohio State players who have finished second in The Heisman Trophy voting.

1-16 How many Big Ten Championships did Woody Hayes win?

1-17 What year and which coach went 11-0 in the regular season and missed the National Championship by losing The Rose Bowl to USC 17-16?

1-18 Fullback Bob White carried the ball seven out of eight plays in a 66-yard game-winning drive to give Ohio State a Big Ten Title and a Rose Bowl trip over what team?

1-19 What was the score of the 1969 Rose Bowl game when Ohio State beat No. 1 USC Heisman Trophy winner O.J. Simpson and won the National Championship?

1-20 Archie Griffin (in his second game as a freshman) came off the bench, rushed for an Ohio State record of how many yards, and against what team?

ANSWERS GROUP 1

1-1   The Ohio Stadium

1-2   Brutus Buckeye

1-3   1951-1978

1-4   True

1-5   2003

1-6   1918

1-7   Woody Hayes vs. Bo Schembechler (1969-1978)

1-8   Block O

1-9   Dotting the "i" in Script Ohio

1-10   Michigan Game 1969, UM 24-OSU 12, OSU was a 17 point favorite

1-11   Jim Stillwagon

1-12   Southeast corner tower of Ohio Stadium

1-13   Over 35 million and quickly going to 36 million

1-14   Two-time All-American Bob Ferguson

1-15   Bob Ferguson (1961), John Hicks (1973), Keith Byars (1984)

1-16   13

1-17   1979, Head Coach Earle Bruce

1-18   Iowa, November 16, 1957

1-19   Ohio State 27, University of Southern California 16

1-20   239 yards, North Carolina, won 29-14, September 30, 1972

QUESTIONS **GROUP 2**

2-1 What year(s) did Woody Hayes claim the wire service National Championship?

2-2 Because the OSU vs. Michigan rivalry with Bo and Woody was so dominant in The Big Ten Conference, what was the conference called?

2-3 What year did Ohio State add the player's name on the back of their jersey?

2-4 The Ohio Stadium is located on the banks of what river?

2-5 How many Rose Bowl games did Woody Hayes' teams play in?

2-6 Who caught Craig Krensel's pass, the "Holy Buckeye," at Purdue in 2002?

2-7 **T or F** Michigan was always unbeaten going into the Ohio State game from 1972 through 1975 and only beat the Buckeyes once.

2-8 What was coach Woody Hayes' record against Michigan in 28 games?

2-9 Name the two Ohio State linebackers with the most tackles in a game.

2-10 What was the title of Woody Hayes' book published in 1969?

2-11 Name the three colleges where Woody Hayes was the head coach?

2-12 What band played the 1965 rock hit "Hang on Sloopy"?

2-13 Coach John Cooper (OSU's 21st head coach) had what record after 11 seasons?

2-14 Which game did LB Chris Spielman state was his best game?

2-15 What position did Woody Hayes play at Denison University?

2-16 Which bowl game in 1950 did Coach Hayes beat Arizona State 34-21 with his Miami of Ohio team?

2-17 Who is the "Neutron Man," known as the icon to Ohio State Football?

2-18 Where is the "Coffin Corner(s)" in Ohio Stadium?

2-19 In what year and against which opponent did the Ohio State Buckeyes play their first overtime game?

2-20 How many National Championships did Coach Jim Tressel have at Youngstown State University?

ANSWERS GROUP 2

2-1 1954, 1957, 1968

2-2 "Big 2, Little 8"

2-3 1968

2-4 The Olentangy River

2-5 Eight (including four straight from 1972-1975)

2-6 Michael Jenkins

2-7 False: they tied 10-10 in 1973

2-8 17-11-1

2-9 29 tackles, Chris Spielman (Michigan 1986), Tom Cousineau (Penn State 1978)

2-10 *Hot Line to Victory*

2-11 Denison University (1946-1948), Miami University of Ohio (1949-1950), The Ohio State University (1951-1978)

2-12 The McCoys

2-13 111-43-4

2-14 Iowa 1985, 2 interceptions, 19 tackles

2-15 Tackle

2-16 Salad Bowl

2-17 Mr. Orlas King (passed away 10-7-2004)

2-18 Both ends of the playing field between the goal line and the 10-yard line

2-19 2002, Illinois, Ohio State won 23-16

2-20 Four

QUESTIONS GROUP 3

3-1 **T or F** Coach Cooper's players won the Butkus, Heisman, Lombardi, Outland and Thrope Awards.

3-2 Since 1935 the last regular season game has been with which opponent?

3-3 In honor of every OSU All-American since 1934, what is planted in "The Buckeye Grove" on the south side of Ohio Stadium?

3-4 Which head coach was an honorary "i" dotter?

3-5 What year did the "Super Sophomores" win a national championship for the Buckeyes?

3-6 John Hicks, as a senior tackle, won which two national awards?

3-7 Coach Woody Hayes referred to Michigan as what?

3-8 What was Head Coach Woody Hayes' record while coaching at Ohio State?

3-9 Who holds the record for the most rushing yards in a single game in the Horseshoe?

3-10 How many 400-yard passing games has Ohio State produced through 2004?

3-11 What is the title of the DVD about the life and times of Woody Hayes?

3-12 Who is the only kicker to win the team MVP Award?

3-13 Jack Nicklaus and Jesse Owens from Ohio State have been on the Wheaties cereal box cover. Which Big Ten coaching legend has also been so honored?

3-14 Coach Woody Hayes really had only one true peer during his coaching tenure at Ohio State, who was it?

3-15 Ohio State had five coaches in a period of eleven years. What was that time known as?

3-16 Who was voted by ESPN in 1999 as the nation's No. 1 college football recruiter?

3-17 When was coach Woody Hayes' birthday?

3-18 **T or F** Coach Hayes' Buckeye team twice won a conference-record 17 consecutive league games.

3-19 Ohio State is the only Big Ten team to play in four consecutive Rose Bowl games. Which four seasons did Woody Hayes' team accomplish this feat?

3-20 Which Heisman Trophy Award winners wore the following numbers? #22, #40, #31, #27, #45, and #10

ANSWERS GROUP 3

3-1 True

3-2 The Michigan "Wolverines"

3-3 A Buckeye tree

3-4 Woody Hayes

3-5 The 1968 team

3-6 Lombardi Trophy and Outland Award

3-7 "That State up North" or "That Team up North"

3-8 1951-1978, 205-68-10, .761 winning percentage

3-9 Eddie George, 314 yards on 36 carries vs. Illinois, 1995

3-10 One, 458 yards against Florida State in 1981

3-11 *Beyond the Gridiron*

3-12 Mike Nugent, 2004

3-13 Joe Paterno, Penn State

3-14 Coach Bear Bryant, Alabama

3-15 "Graveyard of Coaches," Woody Hayes was hired and changed all of that!

3-16 Coach Bill Conley

3-17 Valentine's Day, February 14, 1913

3-18 True

3-19 1972, 1973, 1974, and 1975

3-20 Les Horvath (1944) #22, Howard "Hopalong" Cassady (1955) #40, Vic Janowicz (1950) #31, Eddie George (1995) #27, Archie Griffin (1974-75) #45, Troy Smith (2006) #10

QUESTIONS GROUP 4

4-1 **T or F** In 1970 Ohio State was the National Football Foundation National Champion.

4-2 Coach John Cooper's last loss in the 2001 Outback Bowl to South Carolina was to which former Ohio State assistant football coach?

4-3 Which game is considered Ohio State's best victory ever?

4-4 **T or F** The Ohio Stadium, "The Horseshoe," is listed in the National Registry of Historic Buildings.

4-5 Who stripped the Miami Hurricanes' Sean Taylor's interception and once again turned the momentum of the 2003 Fiesta Bowl National Championship Game?

4-6 Who was the last team to join The Big Ten Football Conference?

4-7 How many total victories did Coach Woody Hayes have as a college coach?

4-8 "Insight & Inspiration from Coach Earle Bruce" was the bi-line for his book titled what?

4-9 What does W.W. stand for in W.W. (Woody) Hayes' name?

4-10 What is the prestigious award that recognizes excellence in academics, athletics and community service?

4-11 What are the two Athletic Hall of Fames of which Coach Woody Hayes is a member?

4-12 Who was the first Ohio State Heisman Trophy winner to play major league baseball?

4-13 **T or F** Coach Bo Schembechler was an assistant coach to Woody Hayes during two different periods.

4-14 **T or F** The Big Ten representative from 1968 through 1980 (13 seasons) was either Ohio State or UM.

4-15 What is the "Skull Session?"

4-16 Which two running backs have scored five touchdowns in a single game?

4-17 What year did the Buckeyes outscore their opponents 40.2 to 7.8 and no other team came within four touchdowns of Ohio State going into the Michigan game?

4-18 Who was *The Columbus Dispatch* endorsing for the head coaching job at Ohio State in 1951?

4-19 Which Oklahoma kicker won the 1977 game 29-28 with a 41-yard field goal after the Buckeyes came back from being down 20-0 and leading 28-20?

4-20 What game cancelled Leroy Keyes' Heisman Trophy run and his team's No. 1 ranking?

ANSWERS GROUP 4

4-1   True

4-2   Lou Holtz

4-3   National Championship Game 2002, OSU 31-Miami 24 (2 OT)

4-4   True: on March 22, 1974 by the National Park Service

4-5   Maurice Clarett

4-6   Penn State

4-7   241

4-8   *Buckeye Wisdom*

4-9   Wayne Woodrow

4-10 Woody Hayes National Scholar Athlete Award

4-11 Denison Athletic Hall of Fame and College Football Hall of Fame

4-12 Vic Janowicz

4-13 True: 1952-53 (Graduate Assistant) and 1959-1963 (Assistant)

4-14 True

4-15 A concert/pep rally by the Ohio State Marching Band in St. John Arena. They start two hours before kickoff at home games.

4-16 Pete Johnson (1974 vs. North Carolina), Keith Byars (1984 vs. Illinois)

4-17 1969, but Ohio State lost 24-12

4-18 Paul Brown of the Cleveland Browns

4-19 Uwe Von Schamann

4-20 1968, Purdue, 13-0 Ohio State in the "Horseshoe"

QUESTIONS GROUP 5 *Vintage*

5-1 Who holds the Ohio State record of 10 extra points in a single game?

5-2 Who had the longest running play and did not score a touchdown in Ohio State history?

5-3 "Senior Tackle" was started in 1913 by which Head Coach?

5-4 Although over 100,000 people have probably said they were at "The Snow Bowl" game, what is the published attendance number?

5-5 Which Head Coach had the nickname "Close the Gates of Mercy?"

5-6 Who holds the rushing record for the most yards gained by a "vintage" player in a single game?

5-7 Who did Ohio State beat 23-3 in 1916 to win their first conference championship and go undefeated?

5-8 What was the "Bad Water Game?"

5-9 During the "Vintage Years" 1890-1950, how many head coaches coached seven years or more at Ohio State?

5-10 What is the least number of points scored by a "vintage" team in a bowl game?

5-11 After retiring, which Head Coach continued his career in medicine and did heart disease research?

5-12 When did Ohio State meet Michigan for the first time with The Big Ten Title on the line?

5-13 What year(s) was the first "Ramp Entrance" and "Script Ohio" by TBDBITL?

5-14 What year did Ohio State finally, after many tries, Beat Michigan?

5-15 Who was Ohio State's first All-American player in 1914?

5-16 T or F Chic Harley only lettered in football as Ohio State's first three-time All-American.

5-17 What was the first game Ohio State played west of the Mississippi River?

5-18 T or F Ohio State has had bad luck in winning "Stadia" games; last game at Ohio Field, Dedication games at Ohio Stadium and Michigan Stadium.

5-19 Who played his last game in the "Horseshoe," and then the next day signed with George Halas and played the last six games of 1925 with the Chicago Bears?

5-20 What "vintage" head coach had three Big Ten Championships, 16 players making All-American, and was inducted into the College Football Hall of Fame?

ANSWERS GROUP 5 *Vintage*

5-1   Vic Janowicz, 1950 vs. Iowa

5-2   Gene Fekete, 89 yards, Pittsburgh 1942

5-3   Head Coach John Wilce

5-4   50,503

5-5   Head Coach Francis Schmidt

5-6   Oliver Cline 1945, 239 yards vs. Pittsburgh

5-7   Northwestern, 1916 under Head Coach John Wilce

5-8   1942 loss at Wisconsin 17-7, when most of the Ohio State players got sick from drinking foul water on the players train, however, they still won Ohio State's first National Championship.

5-9   Two, John Wilce 16 years, Francis Schmidt seven years

5-10   Zero (0) vs. California in 1921 Rose Bowl

5-11   Dr. John Wilce, Head Coach 1913-1928

5-12   1944, Ohio State 18, Michigan 14

5-13   Ramp Entrance 1928; Script Ohio 1936

5-14   1919

5-15   Boyd Cherry

5-16   False: Chic Harley lettered in four sports...basketball, baseball, track and football.

5-17   1920 Rose Bowl, losing to California 28-0

5-18   True: Ohio State lost all three games

5-19   The Legendary Harold "Red" Grange #77

5-20   Head Coach John Wilce

QUESTIONS GROUP 6

6-1   Notre Dame and USC rank first with Heisman Trophy winners. Where does Ohio State rank?

6-2   What years did Coach Woody Hayes serve in the United States Navy?

6-3   "Script Ohio" is played to the rhythmic beat of what song?

6-4   How much does the "Victory Bell" weigh?

6-5   The "Tunnel of Pride" started in 1995 at the Notre Dame game was the idea of what Ex-OSU quarterback?

6-6   Which three assistant coaches for Woody Hayes are enshrined in the College Football Hall of Fame?

6-7   Who made the "Pancake" block famous?

6-8   Who was the first player to win both the Lombardi and Outland trophies in the same season?

6-9   What was head coach Woody Hayes' record in eight Rose Bowl appearances?

6-10   Which head coach won four Big Ten Titles, a Cotton Bowl and Fiesta Bowl, and was 5-4 against UM?

6-11   Which two time All-American is considered Ohio State's best pass rusher to date?

6-12   Which band member dots the "i" in Script Ohio?

6-13   What is the seating capacity of Ohio Stadium after the recent renovation, preservation and expansion?

6-14   Woody Hayes' nickname over time became what?

6-15   **T or F**   Ohio State is the only school to perform "Script Ohio."

6-16   What punter holds the record for the longest punt of 74 yards at Ohio State?

6-17   What was the cost of the three-year renovation project at Ohio Stadium completed in 2001?

6-18   What corporation wanted to buy the rights and rename "The Game" (Ohio State vs. Michigan) for a million dollars in 2004?

6-19   The largest crowd to date (2006) is the 103rd game with Michigan, November 18, 2006 (42-39 OSU). What was the attendance?

6-20   Who said the following? "To be average is to be the lowest of the good and the best of the bad. Who wants to be average?"

ANSWERS GROUP 6

6-1 OSU is tied with USC and Notre Dame; all with seven winners.
6-2 1941-1946
6-3 Le Regiment
6-4 2,420 pounds
6-5 Rex Kern
6-6 Ernie Godfrey, Doyt Perry, and Earle Bruce
6-7 Orlando Pace
6-8 Jim Stillwagon, 1970
6-9 4 - 4
6-10 Earle Bruce (1979-1987)
6-11 Mike Vrabel (1993-1996)
6-12 A sousaphone player, who must be at least a fourth-year band member
6-13 101,568 seats
6-14 "The Old Man"
6-15 False: Michigan did it first, Stanford tried it and misspelled Ohio
6-16 Andy Groom
6-17 $194,000,000.00
6-18 SBC, the offer was declined!
6-19 105,708
6-20 Earle Bruce

QUESTIONS GROUP 7

7-1 Which three former Ohio State players are in the Top 100 Pro Football Players selection?

7-2 Who are members of all three of these: The Ohio High School, College, and Pro Football Hall of Fames?

7-3 What is a "String of Pearls?"

7-4 Head Coach Woody Hayes produced how many All-Americans?

7-5 Who holds the record for the most rushing yards at Ohio State in a single season?

7-6 Who said the following? "That victory...was for our great fans!"

7-7 Who did Ohio State defeat when Keith Byars rushed for a record 274 yards and the team came back from a 24-0 deficit?

7-8 What other Big Ten team also went undefeated in 2002 to share the Big Ten Title with Ohio State?

7-9 Who was the first Ohio State sophomore player to ever win the Lombardi Trophy?

7-10 Who was Ohio State's first two-time All-American linebacker?

7-11 T or F The "Super Sophomores" did not lose a game in "The Horseshoe" for three years.

7-12 Who was the first player to be taken as the first pick in the NFL Draft from Ohio State?

7-13 What was Woody Hayes' worst home defeat at Ohio State?

7-14 Who was Woody Hayes' secondary coach on the 1968 National Championship team?

7-15 Which two All-American tackles did fullback Jim Otis run behind?

7-16 Head coach Jim Tressel played what position at Baldwin-Wallace?

7-17 Which Michigan player "Flaunted" the Heisman Trophy pose in "The Game"?

7-18 Who said the following? "The thing I'm most proud of about my college career is that I played on four teams that never lost to Michigan."

7-19 Who caught Craig Krenzel's winning touchdown pass on 4th-and-1 with 1:36 left to play at Purdue in 2002?

7-20 Who scored the first touchdown for first year Head Coach Woody Hayes in 1951?

ANSWERS GROUP 7

7-1 Lou "the toe" Groza, Jim Parker, and Paul Warfield

7-2 Jim Parker and Bill Willis

7-3 Missed tacklers left in the line of the running back. Archie Griffin was very good at this!

7-4 56

7-5 Eddie George, 1,927 yards, 1995

7-6 John Cooper, 1997 Rose Bowl (Ohio State 20-Arizona State 17)

7-7 Illinois, 1984 (Ohio State 45-Illinois 38)

7-8 Iowa "Hawkeyes"

7-9 Orlando Pace

7-10 Dwight "Ike" Kelly 1964-1965

7-11 True! As a team they were 27-2 for three years

7-12 Tom Cousineau, 1979

7-13 Purdue, 41-6 home loss in 1967

7-14 Lou Holtz

7-15 Dave Foley and Rufus Mayes

7-16 Quarterback

7-17 Desmond Howard, 1991

7-18 Archie Griffin, 1972-1975

7-19 Michael Jenkins

7-20 Robert "Rock" Joslin

QUESTIONS GROUP 8

8-1 Which Wolverine QB has thrown a touchdown pass in Super Bowl #38 and #39 to which former Ohio State Buckeye defensive player?

8-2 What do players and coaches receive following the victories over the Michigan Wolverines?

8-3 The Ohio Stadium is located on what road?

8-4 Who said the following? "You win with people."

8-5 Six of the Top 10 Ohio State records for passing yards in a single game are held by which quarterback?

8-6 Who came through unblocked to block a Michigan punt in the 4th quarter and then the ball was picked up by Todd Bell, who ran it in for the game winning touchdown?

8-7 Buckeye Spirit Song, "We Don't Give a Damn for The Whole State of _____?"

8-8 Which player led the Buckeyes in tackles for three years in the 1990s?

8-9 Who led Ohio State in rushing in 1967, '68 and '69, with career totals of 2,542 yards and 35 touchdowns?

8-10 Jim Otis scored four touchdowns against Michigan in 1968 giving him 16 for the season. Whose record did he break?

8-11 Which two quarterbacks filled "in relief" for Rex Kern when he was hurt during the National Championship run in 1968?

8-12 Which All-American quarterback started 48 consecutive games?

8-13 Who said the following? "He's a better young man than he is a football player, and he's the best football player I've ever seen."

8-14 T or F The Ohio State Buckeyes have been called "Defensive Back U."

8-15 Which quarterback, in his final game against Michigan, threw for 330 yards and three touchdowns?

8-16 Who did play-by-play from 1950 to 1979 for radio, served as assistant SID (1949-1972), and was the Sports Information Director (SID) from 1973 until his retirement in 1987?

8-17 Name the six former Ohio State players in the NFL Hall of Fame.

8-18 Which Ohio State quarterback is the career passing leader in yards?

8-19 T or F Three Ohio State quarterbacks have a career completion percentage over 60%.

8-20 Which two Buckeye quarterbacks have thrown five touchdown passes in a game?

ANSWERS GROUP 8

8-1   Tom Brady and Mike Vrabel

8-2   A gold charm of a pair of football pants

8-3   411 Woody Hayes Drive, Columbus, Ohio 43210

8-4   Woody Hayes, it's the title of his second book

8-5   Joe Germaine, 1997 and 1998

8-6   Jim Laughlin, sending the No. 1 Buckeyes to the Rose Bowl

8-7   Michigan

8-8   Steve Tovar 1990-91-92

8-9   Jim Otis

8-10   Howard "Hopalong" Cassady

8-11   Bill Long and Ron Maciejowski

8-12   Art Schlichter 1978-1981

8-13   Woody Hayes about Archie Griffin

8-14   True: but what about "Wide Receiver U" and replacing Penn State as "Linebacker U"

8-15   Joe Germaine, 1998

8-16   Marv Homan

8-17   Sid Gillman, Lou Groza, Dante Lavelli, Jim Parker, Paul Warfield, and Bill Willis

8-18   Art Schlichter, 7,547 yards, 1978-1981

8-19   False: one quarterback has done it. Troy Smith 63.4%

8-20   Bobby Hoying, (two times) 1994-1995 and John Borton, 1952

QUESTIONS **GROUP 9**

9-1 He won two Lombardi Awards ('95 and '96) and an Outland Trophy ('96) before becoming the No. 1 overall draft pick in the NFL. Who was he?

9-2 By many historians, who is considered the greatest athlete ever at The Ohio State University?

9-3 In what year did the Big Ten Athletic Directors vote to send Ohio State to the Rose Bowl after a 10-10 tie with the undefeated Michigan Wolverines?

9-4 Which All-American Ohio State tackle was the first full-time offensive lineman named to the Pro Football Hall of Fame?

9-5 When is Bo Schembechler's birthday?

9-6 The Ohio State rushing yards record for a career is held by which running back?

9-7 Through 2006, what is Ohio State's home opening game record?

9-8 Who holds the Ohio State record for career interceptions at 22?

9-9 What was the smallest crowd after the 1950 "Snow Bowl?"

9-10 Who said the following? "The greatest defensive effort I've ever seen."

9-11 After winning their fifth Big Ten Title in six years, Columbus was called what?

9-12 What father/son combination were both Co-Captains at Ohio State?

9-13 Of all the wonderful honors Coach Woody Hayes received, what did he consider the greatest?

9-14 Who said the following? "The greatest comeback after the worst start I've ever been associated with."

9-15 Which All-American punter holds the Ohio State punting average record of 45.0 yards on 109 punts?

9-16 Who holds the Ohio State record for the most punt return yardage in a single game?

9-17 **T or F** Art Schlichter was 4th, 6th, and 5th in 1979, 1980 and 1981 in the Heisman Trophy voting.

9-18 Through 2006 when opponents were ranked No. 1, what was Ohio State's win/loss record?

9-19 What is "The Pride of the Buckeyes?"

9-20 Who is the only Buckeye running back to lead his teams in rushing yards in four straight seasons?

ANSWERS GROUP 9

9-1   Orlando Pace

9-2   Vic Janowicz

9-3   1973; Bo was HOT!

9-4   Jim Parker

9-5   April Fools' Day, April 1, 1929

9-6   Archie Griffin, 5,589 yards, 1972-1975

9-7   104-7-4

9-8   Mike Sensibaugh

9-9   11-11-1967, Wisconsin, in a downpour. 65,470 fans

9-10   Woody Hayes after beating No. 1 Purdue 13-0 in 1968

9-11   "The Capital of College Football"

9-12   Jim Herbstreit, 1960 and Kirk Herbstreit, 1992

9-13   Delivering the Commencement Address at Ohio State, March 22, 1986

9-14   Earle Bruce, Illinois 1984, Ohio State won 45-38

9-15   Andy Groom

9-16   Neal Colzie, 170 yards vs. Michigan State 1973

9-17   True

9-18   6 - 9

9-19   The Ohio State University Marching Band. All Brass Band of 225 proud members.

9-20   Archie Griffin

QUESTIONS GROUP 10 *Vintage*

10-1   Who was Ohio State's first three-time All-American?

10-2   On what date was the Ohio Stadium dedicated and who was the opponent that day?

10-3   What was the name of the football field Ohio State played on before building "The Horseshoe?"

10-4   The site where the new Ohio Stadium was to be built was known as what?

10-5   **T or F** Ohio State won the Michigan Stadium dedication game October 22, 1927.

10-6   Which head coach won the first National Football Championship for the Ohio State Buckeyes?

10-7   **T or F** Ohio State did not win the Michigan game until their 16th meeting in 1919.

10-8   The Ohio State fight song "Across the Field" was written as a tribute to which head coach?

10-9   What was the date of the famous "Snow Bowl?"

10-10 Who was Maudine Ormsby?

10-11 Who is credited with being the "Father of the Ohio Stadium" project in the 1920s?

10-12 Which school colors were picked before Scarlet & Gray...as no one had these colors?

10-13 What was the seating capacity of the new Ohio Stadium in 1922?

10-14 Who was the Athletic Director during the construction of the Ohio Stadium?

10-15 Before it was renamed The Ohio Field in 1908, what was the previous football field called?

10-16 Head Coach Wes Fesler's last game was against whom?

10-17 Ohio State's airport on Case Road in Columbus, Ohio is named after which former player?

10-18 Which Ohio State All-American fullback became the Buckeyes' baseball coach from 1951 to 1975?

10-19 Who holds the Ohio State record for the most extra points in a "vintage" game?

10-20 He only played three college games for Head Coach Paul Brown, but he made the NFL Hall of Fame as a Cleveland Brown. Who was he?

ANSWERS GROUP 10 *Vintage*

10-1   Charles Wesley "Chic" Harley 1916, 1917 and 1919

10-2   October 21, 1922, Michigan "Wolverines"

10-3   Ohio Field

10-4   "Cricket Land"

10-5   False: Ohio State lost 21-0

10-6   Paul Brown, 1942

10-7   True

10-8   John Wilce, 1913-1928

10-9   November 25, 1950

10-10 Homecoming Queen 1926, actually she was a Holstein dairy cow

10-11 Professor Thomas French, Engineering Department Chairman

10-12 Orange and Black, but Princeton already had these colors

10-13 66,210

10-14 Lynn St. John

10-15 University Field

10-16 1950 Michigan in "The Snow Bowl," Head Coach Fesler's record was 0-3-1 vs. Michigan

10-17 Don Scott, Quarterback 1938-39-40

10-18 Marty Karow

10-19 Vic Janowicz, 1950 vs. Iowa

10-20 Dante Lavelli, nicknamed "gluefingers"

QUESTIONS GROUP 11

11-1 The Ohio State records for rushing yards in a single game for 1st and 2nd place are held against the same opponent. Who is that opponent?

11-2 The Buckeyes attempted an unusual play for them in the first half of the National Championship Game against the Miami Hurricanes. What was it?

11-3 Which Buckeye holds the records for both single season and career sacks?

11-4 In "The Super Sophomores" class of 1967, how many were drafted into the NFL?

11-5 From 1890, including present day Coach Jim Tressel, how many head coaches has Ohio State had?

11-6 In 1951, when new Head Coach Woody Hayes arrived, he changed the offense from a single wing to what new formation?

11-7 Whose number was the first to be retired in the "Horseshoe?"

11-8 What is the "Illibuck?"

11-9 Who holds the NCAA record with a career average of 6.13 yards per carry?

11-10 What was the title of the bestselling book by Ohio State All-American Jack Tatum?

11-11 Which head coach gave the now famous "310 Days" speech?

11-12 Who said the following? "It's always hard to lose, but I don't mind it as much today because of all you've been through."

11-13 Which Ohio State linebacker is the only winner of the Butkus Award?

11-14 What award is for a lineman (either side of the ball) or a linebacker no further than five yards deep?

11-15 Astro Turf and Super Turf have been two artificial surfaces in the Ohio Stadium. What is the current grass called?

11-16 As of 2004, how many major individual awards have Ohio State players won?

11-17 Name the Ohio State "Band Center" in the Ohio Stadium.

11-18 **T or F** The Buckeye Nut is a shiny, dark brown nut with a light tan patch that resembles the eye of a deer and carrying one brings good luck.

11-19 How many school records did two-time All-American kicker Mike Nugent set in his career?

11-20 How many 100-yard rushing games did Ohio State have in 2004?

ANSWERS GROUP 11

11-1 Illinois, 314 yards 1995, 274 yards 1984

11-2 Fake Field Goal, which failed

11-3 Mike Vrabel, 13 in a single season 1995, 36 career

11-4 13

11-5 22

11-6 T-Formation

11-7 #45 Archie Griffin, 10-30-1999

11-8 A wooden turtle trophy awarded to the Ohio State-Illinois winner since 1925

11-9 Archie Griffin

11-10 *They Call Me Assassin*

11-11 New Head Coach Jim Tressel

11-12 Bo Schembechler to Earle Bruce, after Ohio State upset Michigan 1987

11-13 Andy Katzenmoyer

11-14 Lombardi Award

11-15 FieldTurf, installed in 2007

11-16 30

11-17 Steinbrenner Band Center

11-18 True

11-19 21

11-20 2

QUESTIONS GROUP 12

12-1 **T or F** Linebacker Andy Katzenmoyer lead the team in tackles his sophomore and junior years.

12-2 After the renovation of The Ohio Stadium with 101,568 seats, where does it rank in size in regards to other stadiums?

12-3 Which head coach called the trick play "fumbleroski" in the Michigan game?

12-4 Who said the following? "Coaching is nothing more than eliminating mistakes before you get fired."

12-5 What kicker "hit" four field goals to beat Michigan in 1974, 12-10?

12-6 Who "ran blocked" for Hopalong Cassady, and "pass blocked" for Johnny Unitas?

12-7 The Michigan Stadium is called what?

12-8 What was the "No Repeat" rule?

12-9 Who was the first true freshman to start at running back after World War II?

12-10 What Ohio State running back has the record for the most 100-yard games in a season?

12-11 What does "Old Button Shoe" mean?

12-12 Which Ohio State player won the Fred Bilentnikoff Award for the best collegiate receiver?

12-13 Which Ohio State team had the most All-Americans?

12-14 Who holds the Ohio State record for total offense against Michigan in a single game?

12-15 Which Ohio State Head Coach has scored the most points against Michigan in a game?

12-16 Which Athletic Director at Ohio State played halfback and quarterback at Michigan?

12-17 Since 1950, how many times have Ohio State and Michigan tied (shared) the Big Ten Title?

12-18 Before Woody Hayes won (17-0) at Ann Arbor in 1955, how many years had it been since the last victory for the Buckeyes in Michigan Stadium?

12-19 How many running backs have rushed for over 3000 yards in their careers at Ohio State?

12-20 Who holds the Ohio State record for the most passing yards (3,330) in a single season?

ANSWERS GROUP 12

12-1 False: Katzenmoyer never led the defensive team in tackles

12-2 Fourth. Michigan is first with 107,501 seats, Tennessee second and Penn State third.

12-3 Head Coach Earle Bruce, with Jim Lachey the pulling guard

12-4 Lou Holtz

12-5 Tom Klaban, 47, 25, 43 and 45 yards

12-6 All-American, All-Pro Jim Parker

12-7 "The Big House"

12-8 No team in the Big Ten Conference could go to the Rose Bowl in back-to-back years

12-9 Maurice Clarett

12-10 Eddie George at 12, Archie Griffin twice had 11 games (Archie played fewer games each year)

12-11 T-Formation, with a full house backfield, per coach Woody Hayes

12-12 Terry Glenn, 1995

12-13 1974, DeCree, Schumacher, Cusick, Myers, Griffing, Colzie, and Skladany

12-14 Quarterback Troy Smith, 386 yards, 2004

12-15 Woody Hayes, twice 50 points...1961 and 1968

12-16 Rick Bay, 1961-1964 at the University of Michigan, he did not earn a letter, AD 1984-1987

12-17 Eight times

12-18 18 years...1937 by Francis Schmidt

12-19 Five, Griffin, George, Spencer, Byars and Pearson

12-20 Joe Germaine, 1998

QUESTIONS GROUP 13

13-1   Who said the following? "You've been great, but to be great at Ohio State you've got to Beat Michigan."

13-2   After the 2004 season, who was Ohio State's all-time leading scorer?

13-3   What was Archie Griffin's best overall rushing effort?

13-4   After the 1969 upset loss to Michigan, a custom-made rug was located outside the locker room by head coach Woody Hayes that said what?

13-5   Who said the following? "I think every Buckeye who plays their last game in the Horseshoe leaves something of themselves out there. It's part of playing at Ohio State."

13-6   Jack Nicklaus, the world's greatest golfer went to Pharmacy School at Ohio State. Who is the only player to play in the Rose Bowl and on a National Championship team that is a pharmacist?

13-7   Which of Head Coach Woody Hayes' players is a three-time Academic All-American?

13-8   How many coaches at Ohio State have been inducted into the College Football Hall of Fame?

13-9   What year between 1991 and 1999 did Ohio State not have a first round NFL draft pick?

13-10   Ohio State has had seven Heisman Trophy winners since 1936. How many has Michigan had?

13-11   Which two Ohio State players hold the record for touchdowns (points) in a Michigan game?

13-12   Who was a three year starter at center for Ohio State (1960-62) and head coach at Michigan (1990-94)?

13-13   Which Ohio State team was the first in the NCAA 1A Division to win 14 games in a season?

13-14   Which Ohio State quarterback has the most touchdown passes in a single season?

13-15   How many Ohio State receivers have had 1000 yards in receptions in a single season?

13-16   Which Ohio State player has had three pass interceptions in one game against Michigan?

13-17   **T or F**   The "wolverine" is not a native animal of the State of Michigan.

13-18   Which receiver is the leading career receiver in yardage at Ohio State?

13-19   Which receiver holds the Ohio State record for the most receptions in a career?

13-20   Which two Ohio State rushing backs hold the record for rushing touchdowns in a single game?

ANSWERS GROUP 13

13-1   Earle Bruce, Senior Tackle, 1996
13-2   Kicker Mike Nugent, 356 points
13-3   246 yards, 30 carries, 11-17-1973 vs. Iowa
13-4   1969 Michigan 24, OSU 12, 1970 Mich. ____, OSU____.
13-5   Linebacker Matt Wilhelm, 2002, Ohio State 14, Michigan 9
13-6   Tom Bartley #35, Linebacker 1968, Bartley's Pharmacy, Waverly, Ohio
13-7   Dave Foley, 1966-67-68
13-8   Eight. Jones, Wilce, Schmidt, Godfrey, Hayes, Gillman, Perry, and Bruce
13-9   1998
13-10 Three. Tom Harmon (1940), Desmond Howard (1991) and Charles Woodson (1997)
13-11 24 points, four touchdowns: Bob Ferguson (1961), Jim Otis (1968)
13-12 Gary Moeller, Co-Captain 1962
13-13 2002
13-14 Troy Smith, 30, 2006
13-15 Four. Jenkins (2002), Carter (1986), Glenn (1995), and Boston (1998)
13-16 Fred Bruney, 1952
13-17 True: not a verifiable trapping in the whole state of Michigan
13-18 Michael Jenkins, 2,898 yards, 2000-2003
13-19 David Boston, 191, 1996-1998
13-20 Pete Johnson, North Carolina 1974, Keith Byars, Illinois 1984; five TDs each

QUESTIONS GROUP 14

14-1 Which two Buckeye quarterbacks passed for over 1,000 yards in the same season?

14-2 Who said the following? "This is the greatest team I've ever coached. I never saw a team play so close to perfection. You never let up."

14-3 Who is the only player in Big Ten history to play on three undisputed league champion teams?

14-4 Name the two greatest interceptions returned for touchdowns by Buckeyes in Ohio Stadium.

14-5 Name the only Ohio State kicker to win the Lou Groza Award.

14-6 Where are pictures of current and former Buckeye players displayed in the Ohio Stadium?

14-7 How many interceptions did Rex Kern throw in the 1969 "upset loss" to Michigan?

14-8 What is the individual Ohio State record for total tackles in a Michigan game?

14-9 **T or F** QB Art Schlichter had 50 touchdown passes in his career at Ohio State, and is the most by any quarterback.

14-10 How many quarterbacks have thrown for over 5,000 yards in their career at Ohio State?

14-11 Who is the Ohio State career total offense leader?

14-12 **T or F** There has been a player who averaged over 200 all-purpose yards per game for a single season.

14-13 Which two Ohio State kickers have kicked five field goals in a single game?

14-14 Who holds the record at Ohio State of 211 total tackles in a single season?

14-15 What year did home attendance in the "Horseshoe" pass the "half-a-million" mark?

14-16 Who was the leading tackler on the 2002 National Championship team?

14-17 What was Head Coach John Cooper's 13-year record against Michigan?

14-18 UM running back Tshminanga Biakabutuka, a.k.a. "Tim" rushed for how many yards (a record) to win against Ohio State in 1995?

14-19 UM player Tai Streets caught a 68-yard touchdown pass when Big Ten Defensive Player of the Year Shawn Springs did what?

14-20 Which stadium held the 100th meeting of "The Game" to be played between Ohio State and Michigan?

Go Bucks!™ **BEAT MICHIGAN**®

ANSWERS GROUP 14

14-1 Joe Germaine and Stanley Jackson, 1996

14-2 Woody Hayes, after beating Michigan 17-0 in 1955 for his second consecutive Big Ten Championship

14-3 Bill Jobko, 1954-55-56

14-4 Howard "Hopalong" Cassady, 1954 vs. Wisconsin (88 yards) and Ted Provost, 1968 vs. Purdue (35 yards)

14-5 Mike Nugent, 2004

14-6 Yassenoff Recruit Center

14-7 Four

14-8 29 tackles, Linebacker Chris Spielman, 1986

14-9 False: Joe Germaine (56), Bobby Hoying (57), and Troy Smith (54)

14-10 Seven. Karsatos, Tomczak, Frey, Germaine, Hoying, Schlichter, and Smith

14-11 Art Schlichter, 8,850 yards, 1978-1981

14-12 True: One player, Keith Byars, 2,448 yards, 1984 average 203.8 all-purpose yards per game

14-13 Bob Atha, Indiana 1981 and Mike Nugent, North Carolina State 2004

14-14 Tom Cousineau, 1978

14-15 1964, 583,740, seven games average 83,391

14-16 Matt Wilhelm

14-17 2-10-1

14-18 313 yards

14-19 "Slipped"

14-20 Michigan Stadium, November 22, 2003

QUESTIONS GROUP 15 *Vintage*

15-1   Who kicked the "Fifth-Quarter" field goal to beat Illinois 29-26 in 1943?

15-2   When did the Ohio State goal posts get torn down for the first time?

15-3   Which head coach resigned because of "the tension brought about by the tremendous desire to win football games?"

15-4   Who was the best Big Ten team in the 1930s with back-to-back Big Ten Championships and also did not lose a home game for seven seasons?

15-5   The Big Ten Conference once denied Ohio State a Rose Bowl trip because of what?

15-6   The winning point margin of 292-6 was established by what team?

15-7   **T or F** The great Buckeye Tradition of Gold Pants, Buckeye Grove, Captain's Breakfast and Block O all started in the 1930s during Francis Schmidt's term as Head Coach.

15-8   What year did Ohio State and Michigan play their first Big Ten Conference game?

15-9   Who was Ohio State's first, colorful, high-strutting, showman Drum Major?

15-10   When did the Ohio Stadium scholarship dorms start?

15-11   **T or F** Ohio State beat The University of Chicago and the first Heisman Trophy winner Jay Berwanger in 1935.

15-12   Who was Ohio State's first, first round draft pick in professional football?

15-13   Which two consecutive years did a "vintage" Ohio State team win the Big Ten Title outright?

15-14   How many tries did it take for Ohio State to Beat Michigan for the first time?

15-15   "Hopalong" Cassady is known as the spark that started to make football at Ohio State "the way we know it today." Who was the spark to really get Ohio State football started in the beginning?

15-16   Illinois upset Ohio State in 1921, and came away with what nickname?

15-17   **T or F** One of the "Four Horseman" from the famous Notre Dame backfield coached at Ohio State.

15-18   **T or F** Michigan is the only Big Ten team to wear the famous "flying wing" helmet.

15-19   Who was the Big Ten head coach for 29 years that took his worst beating (40-0) from Ohio State?

15-20   Who was Ohio State's first opponent and in what year did they play?

ANSWERS GROUP 15 *Vintage*

15-1   Paul Stungis

15-2   1934 Michigan game, Ohio State winning 34-0

15-3   Wes Fesler 1947-1950, followed by Woody Hayes 1951-1978

15-4   Minnesota

15-5   1944, based on WWII travel regulations and restrictions

15-6   1917, with Chic Harley

15-7   True

15-8   1918

15-9   Edwin "Tubby" Essington 1920-1922

15-10 During the Great Depression to help students with housing, relocated in 2001

15-11 True: 20-13

15-12 Halfback James McDonald by the Philadelphia Eagles, 1938

15-13 1916-1917

15-14 16 tries, Buckeyes won 13-3 at Ann Arbor October 25, 1919

15-15 Chic Harley, recognized by Harley's Rock on High Street at Woodruff Avenue

15-16 "Fighting Illini"

15-17 True, Don Miller 29-32

15-18 False: several Big Ten schools did during the 1930s, including Ohio State

15-19 Bob Zuppke from Illinois, 1931

15-20 Ohio Wesleyan in 1890, Ohio State 20-Ohio Wesleyan 14

QUESTIONS GROUP 16

16-1 Since 1935, through 2006, how many times has "The Game" decided the Big Ten Champion?

16-2 Since 1935, through 2006, how many times has "The Game" had a direct affect determining the Big Ten Champion?

16-3 In 1998, how many games did quarterback Joe Germaine gain 300-plus yards in total offense?

16-4 In the 90s, Ohio State was the number one producer of NFL talent. How many players were taken in the first round of the NFL draft?

16-5 What is the title of the primary Ohio State fight song?

16-6 How many of Head Coach Woody Hayes' teams shut-out Michigan?

16-7 What year did Ohio State set records for rushing yards, attempts and touchdowns against Michigan?

16-8 Which Ohio State player has won "The Jim Thrope Award" for best defensive back?

16-9 Who came off the bench as a freshman, scored three touchdowns in his first game, and started every game thereafter?

16-10 Where is the College Football Hall of Fame museum located?

16-11 Who kicked the 34-yard winning field goal in the 1958 Rose Bowl (OSU vs. Oregon)?

16-12 How long was the winning streak of the Miami Hurricanes before the Buckeyes broke it in the 2002 National Championship Fiesta Bowl game?

16-13 What new tradition did Head Coach Jim Tressel start after every game...win or lose?

16-14 In 1985, a State of Ohio "House Resolution" named what song as Ohio's rock song?

16-15 The Big Ten Athlete of the Year is named for whom?

16-16 What are "The Silver Bullets?"

16-17 Who said the following? "Three things can happen when you pass, and two of them are bad."

16-18 Which Buckeye won the "Ray Guy Award" for being an outstanding punter?

16-19 What two years did Ohio State place eleven players on the All-Big Ten Team?

16-20 Which Heisman Trophy winning quarterback upset Ohio State in the 1971 Rose Bowl?

ANSWERS GROUP 16

16-1   21 times

16-2   23 times

16-3   Five

16-4   15 of Coach John Cooper's players

16-5   "Buckeye Battle Cry" is played when the band enters the stadium and after every touchdown

16-6   Three times. 1955, 1960 and 1962

16-7   1968, 421 yards, 79 attempts and seven touchdowns

16-8   Antoine Winfield, 1998

16-9   Howard "Hopalong" Cassady

16-10 111 South St. Joseph Street, South Bend, Indiana 46601. 1-800-440-3263

16-11 Don Sutherin, Ohio State 10-Oregon 7

16-12 34 games

16-13 The singing of "Carmen Ohio" in the End Zone to the Ohio State Marching Band

16-14 "Hang on Sloopy"

16-15 Started in 1982. Jesse Owens Athlete of the Year Award

16-16 The Ohio State Defensive Team

16-17 Woody Hayes

16-18 B.J. Sander, 2003

16-19 1969 and 1975

16-20 Jim Plunkett, Stanford 27-17

QUESTIONS **GROUP 17**

17-1   Who gained 400 yards in total offense in a single game for the Buckeyes?

17-2   Who holds the record for career all-purpose yards gained per game at Ohio State?

17-3   Who lead the nation in 2004 with five field goals over 50 yards long?

17-4   Who holds the record for solo tackles in a career at Ohio State?

17-5   Which year did Ohio State's total season attendance go over 1,000,000 fans?

17-6   Who said the following? "I don't know how I could ever have a win bigger than this one."

17-7   Which Ohio State head coach received a three-year contract extension on the same day he lost his fourth straight game to Michigan?

17-8   Being indoctrinated into the Ohio State Marching Band "Michigan Hate Club," you are told what quote?

17-9   Who is the only Ohio State player to start four consecutive Rose Bowls?

17-10 How many of Woody Hayes' players have been inducted into The College Football Hall of Fame?

17-11 Name Archie Griffin's two brothers that played at Ohio State.

17-12 Who is the only non-linebacker to have 200 solo tackles in his Buckeye career?

17-13 Who kicked three field goals and two extra points for the 1955 College All-Stars to upset the Cleveland Browns 30-27?

17-14 In what four-year period did Head Coach Wood Hayes win three Big Ten Titles and two National Championships?

17-15 Kicking more field goals was encouraged starting in what season, by widening the goal post to 24 feet?

17-16 What was Head Coach Woody Hayes record against Northwestern coach Ara Parseghian before Ara moved on to Notre Dame?

17-17 Notre Dame returned to Columbus in 1995 after 60 years absence since "The Game of the Century" to what result?

17-18 Which player on the 2002 National Championship team played offense, defense, and special teams?

17-19 When Jim Tressel breaks this coaches' record, who was the coach who had been the second most-winning head coach at Ohio State?

17-20 **T or F**   From 1972 to 1977, Woody Hayes' teams won or shared six Big Ten Titles.

ANSWERS GROUP 17

17-1   Art Schlichter, 1981

17-2   Archie Griffin, 145.8 yards per game, 6,558 yards, 1972-1975

17-3   Mike Nugent

17-4   Chris Spielman, 283 solo tackles, 1984-1987

17-5   1975

17-6   Lloyd Carr, rookie head-coaching year at Michigan in 1995, remember "Bo" in 1968?

17-7   John Cooper

17-8   "Michigan is north until you smell it and west until you step in it."

17-9   Archie Griffin

17-10 11

17-11 Duncan and Ray Griffin

17-12 Antoine Winfield

17-13 Tad Weed

17-14 1954 through 1957

17-15 1959

17-16 1 - 3

17-17 Notre Dame losing 45 to 26

17-18 Chris Gamble

17-19 Head Coach John Cooper

17-20 True: five ties, one outright in 1975

QUESTIONS GROUP 18

18-1 What team posted the first-ever Division 1A record of 14-0?

18-2 How many ties have the Ohio State Buckeyes and Michigan Wolverines had?

18-3 What was Woody's greatest offensive showing in a bowl game?

18-4 Head Coach John Cooper led his Buckeyes to 11 bowl games during his tenure. How many did he win?

18-5 In nine seasons, what was Head Coach Earle Bruce's record?

18-6 Name two Ohio State football players that made the "Wheaties" box cover.

18-7 Who won the first Buckeye Leaf Award (sticker) for outstanding play?

18-8 Name the six Ohio State Heisman Trophy Award winners.

18-9 Which 1950 alumnus and comic strip artist drew the original design of the Ohio State Buckeye Leaf?

18-10 Which kicker hit five 50-yard field goals in his career and tied a record of five field goals in one game during a single season?

18-11 Which two buildings (structures) greatly influenced the design of The Ohio Stadium?

18-12 What was the title of the most successful song The Beatles ever released when the Buckeyes were also No. 1 in 1968?

18-13 The house that "The Babe" built was Yankee Stadium. Who caused The Ohio Stadium "house" to be built?

18-14 Which running back holds the records for the most yards in a single game (314), and the most yards in a single season (1,927)?

18-15 TBDBITL is an acronym for what?

18-16 What year did Brutus Buckeye first appear?

18-17 Where is the James Cleveland Memorial statue?

18-18 What year celebrated the 125th year of college football, which started with Rutgers vs. Princeton?

18-19 **T or F** Woody Hayes, Ara Parseghian, and Bo Schembechler all coached at "The Cradle of Coaches."

18-20 Head Coach Earle Bruce was a head coach at what two colleges before he came to Ohio State in 1979?

ANSWERS **GROUP 18**

18-1   2002 Ohio State National Champion Buckeyes

18-2   Six. 1900, 1910, 1941, 1949, 1973, and 1992

18-3   1975 Rose Bowl, Ohio State 42-USC 21

18-4   Three

18-5   81-26-1

18-6   Tom Matte and Chris Spielman

18-7   Jim Nein (#9), 1967

18-8   Les Horvath (1944), Vic Janowicz (1950), "Hopalong" Cassady (1955), Archie Griffin (1974-1975), Eddie George (1995), and Troy Smith (2006)

18-9   Milton Caniff

18-10   Two-time All-American Kicker Mike Nugent

18-11   Pantheon and Roman Coliseum

18-12   "Hey Jude"

18-13   "Chic" Harley

18-14   Eddie George, 1995 Heisman Trophy winner

18-15   "The Best Damn Band in the Land"

18-16   1965

18-17   The James Cleveland (Jesse Owens) Memorial is located outside Ohio Stadium at the north entrance.

18-18   1994

18-19   True: Miami University of Ohio

18-20   University of Tampa and Iowa State University

QUESTIONS GROUP 19

19-1 During "Michigan Week," what is the big ritual that students partake in on Thursday night?

19-2 Composer John Philip Sousa called what song "college's best fight song?"

19-3 The Outland Trophy and the Vince Lombardi Award for honoring lineman has been won twice by which two Ohio State players?

19-4 Who was the nickel back that intercepted UM's John Navarre's pass to Braylon Edwards to insure victory (14 to 9) in 2002 and a trip to the Fiesta Bowl National Championship Game?

19-5 How many three-time All-Americans did Head Coach Wood Hayes have play for him?

19-6 Which Buckeye won the Dave Rimmington Trophy for the Outstanding Center in 2001?

19-7 **T or F** Woody Hayes had at least one All-Big Ten Player every year for twenty-eight years.

19-8 What year (season) was the two-point extra point option added after a touchdown?

19-9 Which Ohio State quarterback had the most pass completions in a single season?

19-10 Which head coach had a better winning percentage, Earle Bruce or John Cooper?

19-11 Which Ohio State lineman finished second in the Heisman Trophy voting in 1973?

19-12 Which OSU QB made his first start at UM and won the game for the first time in Ann Arbor since 1987?

19-13 What year did only three Ohio State players get drafted into the NFL, but all three went to the same team, the Cleveland Browns?

19-14 In which bowl game has Ohio State had their most touchdown passes?

19-15 John Cooper's 100th victory came with one second left on the clock, with a pass reception by whom?

19-16 Who holds the record for the most rushing yards per game for a single season at Ohio State and who holds the record for the most rushing yards for a career?

19-17 Who holds the Ohio State record for most pass receptions in a single game?

19-18 Who punted for over 5½ miles in yards during his career at Ohio State?

19-19 Which two athletic facilities were named after the two gentlemen most responsible for the construction of the Ohio Stadium?

19-20 In which game did Ohio State stop their opponent on the six-inch yard line, then drive the distance of the field to score the winning touchdown?

ANSWERS GROUP 19

19-1   Jumping into Mirror Lake

19-2   "The Victors," The University of Michigan

19-3   John Hicks (1973) and Orlando Pace (1996)

19-4   Will Allen

19-5   Two. Archie Griffin and Tom Skladany

19-6   Le Charles Bentley

19-7   True

19-8   1958

19-9   Joe Germaine, 230, 1998

19-10 Earle Bruce .755 vs. .702

19-11 John Hicks, 1973 to Jon Cappelletti of Penn State

19-12 Craig Krenzel, 2001

19-13 1960. Jim Marshall, Jim Houston, and Bob White

19-14 Four. 2004 Fiesta Bowl vs. Kansas State

19-15 Bobby Olive

19-16 Eddie George (148.2) 1995 and Archie Griffin (117.3) 1972-1975

19-17 David Boston. 14 vs. Penn State 1997

19-18 Brent Bartholomew, 9,927 yards, 1995-1998

19-19 St. John Arena (L.W. St. John AD) and French Field House (Professor Thomas E. French)

19-20 Michigan game 1954, 21-7

QUESTIONS GROUP 20 *Vintage*

20-1 Who is the only head coach in Ohio State history to start 2-0 against Michigan before 1950?

20-2 WBNS-TV in Columbus, Ohio aired the first coach's show in the country. Who was the coach?

20-3 Which All-American served in World War I (1918)?

20-4 What was the contract price for the construction of The Ohio Stadium in 1921?

20-5 Who was the architect for The Ohio Stadium project?

20-6 Who holds the record for the longest kick-off return of 103 yards for Ohio State?

20-7 Who is the only head coach to shut-out Michigan four years in a row?

20-8 Name the three NFL Hall of Fame players on the original Cleveland Browns team in 1947 that played at Ohio State.

20-9 He was a two-time All-American at end (1932-33), coached 21 years in college, head coach of NFL Los Angeles Rams and AFL San Diego Chargers winning division titles. Who is he?

20-10 Why did Michigan coach Fritz Crisler introduce the "yellow wing" helmet in the 1930s?

20-11 Who holds the record for the most punt attempts in a single game?

20-12 Which Michigan player gave the greatest performance in an Ohio State game when he was 11 for 12 in passing for 151 yards and two touchdowns, ran for 139 yards and two touchdowns, intercepted three passes, kicked four extra points and averaged 50 yards per punt?

20-13 Which famous Michigan coach pronounced Michigan with his southern drawl as "Meechigan?"

20-14 **T or F** James Thurber, OSU grad, humorist, writer, and artist never designed an Ohio State football program.

20-15 What year was the Ohio State vs. Michigan game moved to the final week of conference play?

20-16 Who was the great innovator, credited with the idea for the Super Bowl, the AFC-NFL World Championship?

20-17 He played with "Chic" Harley, then coached the Columbus Tigers pro team in 1922. Who was he?

20-18 Before they played in The Big Ten Conference, what conference did Ohio State play in?

20-19 Which team in 1935 scored three touchdowns in the 4th quarter to overcome a 13-0 score to win 18-13?

20-20 Who was the first Ohio State player to be All-Big Ten in three consecutive seasons?

ANSWERS GROUP 20 *Vintage*

20-1   Head Coach Francis Schmidt, in fact he went 4 - 0 1934-1937

20-2   Head Coach Wes Fesler, 1948

20-3   "Chic" Harley

20-4 $1,341,017.00 to E.H. Latham Co., Columbus, Ohio. Final cost $1,488,168.00

20-5   Howard Dwight Smith, won the gold medal from AIA for "Excellence in Public Work"

20-6   Dean Sensanbaugher, 1943

20-7   Francis Schmidt 1934-35-36-37

20-8   Lou Groza, Dante Lavelli, and Bill Willis

20-9   Sid Gillman

20-10 So the quarterback could distinguish his receivers in the early days of the "forward pass"

20-11 Vic Janowicz, 21, Michigan 1950

20-12 Tom Harmon, 1940, Two-time All-American, Heisman Trophy Award Winner

20-13 Head Coach Fielding Yost

20-14 False: Ohio State vs. Michigan, November 21, 1936 (Homecoming). Only cover he did.

20-15 1935

20-16 Sid Gillman

20-17 All-American Pete Stinchcomb

20-18 Western Conference

20-19 Notre Dame

20-20 Wes Fesler 1928-29-30 and "Chic" Harley did it 1916-17 and 1919

QUESTIONS GROUP 21

21-1 Which Ohio State running back won the Doak Walker Award, Maxwell Award, Walter Camp Player of the Year, and Heisman Trophy in one year?

21-2 Which Buckeye football players have won the Big Ten Athlete of the Year Award?

21-3 Who caught the winning touchdown pass from Joe Germaine in the 1997 Rose Bowl?

21-4 What former Ohio State quarterback became a Major League Baseball pitcher?

21-5 What is Ohio State's record for bowl games from 1920 through 2006?

21-6 T or F Woody Hayes won eight out of ten Michigan games from 1954 until 1964.

21-7 What team won a Big Ten Title in 1995 and shared one in 1996 when they did not play Ohio State?

21-8 What were the most points scored by the Buckeyes in a bowl game?

21-9 Name the father and son who both had key interceptions in the "Horseshoe."

21-10 Who holds the season and career records for the most rushing touchdowns?

21-11 What is the latest example of the Heisman jinx?

21-12 Ernie Godfrey, a National Football Foundation Hall of Fame member, coached how many years at Ohio State?

21-13 What is the greatest comeback victory in Ohio State history?

21-14 Through 2006, what is Ohio State's all-time record when they were No. 1?

21-15 How many 9-3 seasons in a row did Head Coach Earle Bruce have at Ohio State?

21-16 T or F Head Coaches Woody Hayes and John Cooper both had five seasons with ten or more victories.

21-17 How many 200-yard rushing games did Archie Griffin have in his Ohio State career?

21-18 In 1969, fullback Jim Otis became the first 1,000-yard running back. How many has Ohio State had since?

21-19 What year was Woody Hayes' Ohio State team put on probation for "irregularities?"

21-20 The 1975 win at Michigan (21-14) stopped Michigan's consecutive home win record at what number?

ANSWERS GROUP 21

21-1   Eddie George, 1995
21-2   Eddie George, 1996 and Troy Smith, 2006
21-3   David Boston
21-4   Joe Sparma
21-5   18 - 20
21-6   True: only loss in 1956 and 1959
21-7   Northwestern
21-8   47 points vs. BYU in 1982 Holiday Bowl
21-9   Howard "Hopalong" Cassady and his son Craig Cassady
21-10   Pete Johnson (25), 1975 and career (56) 1973-1976
21-11   2007 BCS Championship Game
21-12   33 years
21-13   31-0 deficit to win 41-37 at Minnesota, 1989
21-14   63-9-1
21-15   Six. 1980-1985
21-16   True: although most of Woody Hayes' seasons were nine games and John Cooper's were 12 games.
21-17   Two. 239 yards first game, 246 yards vs. Iowa 1973
21-18   23 total, including Jim Otis
21-19   1956
21-20   41

QUESTIONS GROUP 22

22-1 One of Columbus' most famous addresses is Woody Hayes' home. What is the address?

22-2 Lame duck Head Coach Earle Bruce was supported by his players in his final game against Michigan in 1987 by displaying what?

22-3 Which Ohio State freshman tied the NCAA record with four punt returns for touchdowns?

22-4 Who said the following? "I am not trying to win a popularity poll; I'm trying to win football games."

22-5 Which Ohio State team defeated three top five teams, Notre Dame No. 4, Penn State No. 3, and Arizona State No. 2, and finished No. 2 in the national polls?

22-6 What rank in the United States Navy during WWII did Head Coach Woody Hayes achieve?

22-7 Who holds the record for the most rushing yards in a single season at Ohio State?

22-8 Who has the record for the most solo tackles in a career at Ohio State?

22-9 Who was the hero of the 2002 Penn State game with a touchdown, saving tackle from behind, and an interception for a touchdown that helped to send the Buckeyes to the National Championship Game?

22-10 Which kicker won three games with last minute field goals in a single season?

22-11 Which Columbus restaurant used Woody's picture and the ad line "In All the World There's Only One?"

22-12 Who scored twice on 88-yard runs, one from scrimmage and one a kick-off return in a single game?

22-13 **T or F** Since 1951 Ohio State has won three out of four ball games under Hayes, Bruce, Cooper, and Tressel.

22-14 Who was the first receiver to gain over 1,000 yards in a season at Ohio State?

22-15 What did "So they wouldn't storm the castle" mean?

22-16 What three years did the Michigan State Spartans upset Ohio State and destroy their National Championship goals?

22-17 What was the worst "homer" call against Woody Hayes' Buckeyes, which resulted in a 15-yard penalty for "unsportsmanlike conduct" for Woody?

22-18 Who said the following? "Bulletin board material? All Ohio football players don't go to Michigan, only the good ones."

22-19 Who blocked Iowa's Greg Kostrubali's punt for a safety when Ohio State upset No. 1 Iowa in 1985?

22-20 How many points did Ohio State score in the fourth quarter when they beat Michigan 50-20 in 1961?

ANSWERS GROUP 22

22-1   1711 Cardiff Road, Upper Arlington, Ohio 43220

22-2   "EARLE" Headbands

22-3   Ted Ginn Jr., 2004

22-4   Woody Hayes

22-5   1996 Team

22-6   Lt. Commander

22-7   Eddie George, 1,927 yards, 1995

22-8   Chris Spielman, 283, 1984–1987

22-9   Chris Gamble

22-10 Bob Funk, 1965, 23-21 vs. Wisconsin, 11-10 Minnesota, and 9-7 over Michigan

22-11 Jai Lai, now the Buckeye Hall of Fame

22-12 Morris Bradshaw vs. Wisconsin, 1971

22-13 True: actually a little better than 75%

22-14 Chris Carter, 1986, 1,127 yards on 69 receptions

22-15 Woody Hayes would punt on third down, so the opponents would not rush nine men on fourth down

22-16 1972, 1974, and 1998

22-17 1971. Michigan's Darden over the back pass interference on Ohio State's Dick Wakefield

22-18 Michigan's quarterback Dennis Franklin, 1972. Oh, Michigan lost that game!

22-19 Sonny Gordon

22-20 29 points

QUESTIONS GROUP 23

23-1 How many times during the Ohio State vs. Michigan rivalry have both teams had a losing season?

23-2 Who is the career leader in "sacks" for the Buckeyes?

23-3 **T or F** One time only has Ohio State lost four consecutive bowl games.

23-4 Which Ohio State quarterback had the most yards passing in a season and in a career?

23-5 Who said the following? "Help young people as someone helped you when you were young. Invest in the future."

23-6 Who were the "men of brutality?"

23-7 What was Penn State's first year in the Big Ten Conference, making it 11 teams?

23-8 How many No. 1 teams did Head Coach Earle Bruce defeat?

23-9 Linebacker Jim Laughlin blocked the punt; who ran it in from 18 yards out for the winning touchdown at Michigan 1979?

23-10 Howard "Hopalong" Cassady was what team's worst nightmare?

23-11 The 235-member Michigan Marching Band has what for its trademark formation?

23-12 What "Super Sophomore" was the MVP of the 1969 Rose Bowl Game?

23-13 Who carried the ball 11 of 14 plays in an 80-yard drive to beat Big Ten Champion Iowa 38-28 in 1958?

23-14 Name the leading pass catcher with four receptions for 50 yards in 1955.

23-15 Who is the single season and career kickoff returner at Ohio State?

23-16 **T or F** Chris Carter caught more passes in 1986 than any of Woody Hayes' leading receivers totaled together from 1954 through 1960.

23-17 Which Ohio State linebacker had over 200 total tackles in a season?

23-18 Which Ohio State defensive back twice had three interceptions in a game?

23-19 What is the longest passing play in Ohio State history?

23-20 How many "National Coach of the Year" Awards did Head Coach Woody Hayes win?

ANSWERS GROUP 23

23-1   Once in 1959, Ohio State 3-5-1, Michigan 4-5

23-2   Mike Vrabel (36), 1993-1996

23-3   False: Woody Hayes' last two and Earle Bruce's first two; John Cooper's 1990-1993 teams

23-4   Joe Germaine 3,330 yards, 1998 and Art Schlichter 7,547 yards, 1978-1981

23-5   Woody Hayes. "You can never pay back, but you can always pay forward."

23-6   Defensive backs for Head Coach Earle Bruce

23-7   1993

23-8   One. Iowa 1985, 22-13

23-9   Todd Bell...then on to the Rose Bowl as Big Ten Champions

23-10   Wisconsin...always a Buckeye Victory

23-11   A big capital block "M"

23-12   Quarterback Rex Kern

23-13   Fullback Bob White, overall 209 yards rushing, three touchdowns

23-14   Bill Michael

23-15   Ken-Yon Rambo 1997-2000

23-16   True: 69 vs. 67

23-17   Chris Spielman, 205, 1986 and Tom Cousineau, 244, 1978

23-18   Fred Bruney, Illinois 1951 and Michigan 1952, 17 total interceptions in his career

23-19   Art Schlichter to Calvin Murray, 86 yards vs. Washington State, 1979

23-20   Three. 1957, 1968 and 1975

QUESTIONS GROUP 24

24-1 Name the three running backs in Woody Hayes T-formation for the 1961 National Champions.

24-2 Two "Goal Line Stands" by the underdog Buckeyes proved to be the deciding factor in beating Michigan in what year?

24-3 **T or F** When Woody Hayes teams were ranked No. 1 he was upset only five times.

24-4 Which team has Ohio State beaten the most over the years?

24-5 **T or F** All the scoring in the "Snow Bowl" came from blocked punts.

24-6 What is the number one selling item for "Fan Spirit" at Ohio State?

24-7 Who is the career punt return yardage leader?

24-8 Who has caught the most passes for Ohio State in a single game?

24-9 Which Ohio State kickoff returner has the most yards in a single game?

24-10 Marcus Marek is first in career total tackles at 572, who is second and third?

24-11 Which season did three Buckeyes finish in the top six voting for the Heisman Trophy won by John Cappelletti of Penn State?

24-12 **T or F** Art Schlichter was never a finalist in the Heisman Trophy voting.

24-13 What was the first year that Ohio State averaged over 80,000 fans, 90,000 fans and 100,000 fans in home attendance?

24-14 What two major football programs from southern schools both have a 3-0 record against the Buckeyes?

24-15 Which former Ohio State player and coach, unranked, upset the fifth ranked Ohio State Buckeyes in "The Horseshoe" in 2000?

24-16 Through 2006, what was the last home opener lost by the Buckeyes?

24-17 Who was the first Ohio State quarterback to throw for 300 yards in two consecutive games?

24-18 Who is the only coach from the Big Ten and the Pac-10 to win a Rose Bowl?

24-19 In what football game do all the proceeds go to The Black Coaches Association?

24-20 Who said the following? "I think that was the finest individual effort I've ever seen by a running back."

ANSWERS GROUP 24

24-1   Paul Warfield, Bob Ferguson, and Matt Snell

24-2   1972

24-3   True: four loses and a 10-10 tie at Michigan in 1973

24-4   Indiana, followed by Illinois and Northwestern

24-5   False: all of Michigan's points did, Ohio State's Vic Janowicz kicked a field goal. Final score Michigan 9-Ohio State 3

24-6   Black baseball cap with Scarlet Block "O", aka "Woody's Hat"

24-7   Ted Ginn Jr.

24-8   David Boston, 14, 1997 vs. Penn State

24-9   Carlos Snow, 213 yards vs. Pittsburgh, 1988

24-10   Tom Cousineau, 569; Chris Spielman 546

24-11   1973: John Hicks 2nd, Archie Griffin 5th and Randy Gradishar 6th

24-12   False: he was 4th 1979, 5th 1981 and 6th in 1980

24-13   1954: 80,000, 1988 90,000 and 2001 100,000

24-14   Florida State and Alabama

24-15   Glen Mason, Minnesota 29-17

24-16   Penn State 19-0, 1978

24-17   Joe Germaine, Illinois, and Minnesota 1998

24-18   Head Coach John Cooper

24-19   Eddie Robinson Football Classic

24-20   John Cooper, about Eddie George's 314 rushing yards against Illinois

QUESTIONS GROUP 25 *Vintage*

25-1 **T or F** Red Grange (Illinois) and Tom Harmon (Michigan), both Heisman Trophy winners, played their last college game in "The Horseshoe."

25-2 During the seasons from 1902 to 1921, which conference did Ohio State play in?

25-3 Who holds the Ohio State record for the most yards punting in a game?

25-4 What is Ohio State's all-time record against Notre Dame?

25-5 "The Perfect Play" was what?

25-6 What year did Ohio State win its first Rose Bowl and who did they defeat?

25-7 During the seasons from 1916 to 1949, how many Big Ten Championships and Co-Championships did Ohio State win?

25-8 Who was Ohio State's first African-American All-American (actually two-time) and first African-American to start for the Pros?

25-9 Which player and former assistant coach has the most pairs of "Gold Pants?"

25-10 How many outright Big Ten Titles did Ohio State win in the "vintage" years?

25-11 What famous coach had an agreement to coach at Ohio State in 1929, but was convinced to stay where he had a contract already in place?

25-12 Who was the first head coach to have a coaching contract longer than a year?

25-13 The rule: "A player could not return in any quarter after being taken out in that same quarter" affected what famous game?

25-14 **T or F** Ara Parseghian played for Head Coach Paul Brown while at Ohio State.

25-15 What head coach in his first year, was coach of the Associated Press No. 2 team, but the "National Civilian Champions?"

25-16 What is a "Grid-Graf?"

25-17 How many of the Kabealo brothers played at Ohio State?

25-18 My dad was an ATO, but he was also a member of the non-fraternity fraternity in the 30s at Smitty's Drugstore at 16th and High Streets. What was this organization's name?

25-19 What Big Ten team was the first Associated Press Mythical National Champion in 1936?

25-20 What period of time was Ohio State called the "Graveyard of Coaches?"

ANSWERS GROUP 25 *Vintage*

25-1 True

25-2 Ohio Athletic Conference

25-3 Vic Janowicz, 685 yards, 1950 "Snow Bowl" vs. Michigan

25-4 3-2

25-5 End-around running play, that went for three touchdowns in Ohio State's win against Northwestern, 1916.

25-6 January 2, 1950, Ohio State beat California 17-14

25-7 Six Championships; two Co-Championships

25-8 Bill Willis

25-9 Esco Sarkkinen

25-10 Six

25-11 Knute Rockne

25-12 Head Coach Francis Schmidt, three years 1934-35-36

25-13 Notre Dame 1935, "Game of the Century"

25-14 False: Ara Parseghian played fullback for Paul Brown at the Great Lakes Naval Training Center "Blue Jackets" vs. Ohio State in 1944

25-15 Head Coach Carroll Widdoes, 1944

25-16 A line drawing depicting all the plays on a football field template

25-17 Four

25-18 Si U.

25-19 Minnesota

25-20 1944-1950

QUESTIONS GROUP 26

26-1 Who is the only barber to cut the hair of head coaches Hayes, Bruce, Cooper, and Tressel?

26-2 How many passes did Troy Smith throw in his freshman year?

26-3 Who said "November is for contenders?"

26-4 Who holds the Big Ten single-season record for interceptions?

26-5 Who was the "Butkus Award" winner that scored a touchdown on a blocked punt in his last home game in 2005?

26-6 Name the five former Ohio State head coaches who have been inducted into the College Football Hall of Fame.

26-7 When was the last year "The Game" was not a sell-out?

26-8 Who was the honoree in 2006 to dot the "i"?

26-9 Besides Ohio State, what other school has won seven Heisman Trophies?

26-10 Who was the 1985 favorite to win the Heisman trophy, but a broken foot caused him to miss most of the season?

26-11 Michigan State upset the #1 Buckeyes 28-24 in 1998. How many points underdog were they?

26-12 Before the 2007 BCS Championship Game, OSU vs. Florida, how many times before had they met?

26-13 In the 1960s, which of the Ohio State vs. Michigan games was delayed for a week?

26-14 How many times have Ohio State vs. Michigan been ranked #1 vs. #2?

26-15 What is the Buckeyes favorite fast food restaurant in Scottsdale, Arizona during bowl games?

26-16 Who was the first Buckeye to win the Thorpe Award as the country's outstanding defensive back?

26-17 How many NFL Hall of Fame members from Ohio State have played for the Cleveland Browns?

26-18 Who was *Columbus Monthly* magazine's 2006 Person of the Year?

26-19 After the 2006 Michigan game, who still holds the record for most yards rushing?

26-20 What player from Columbus West High School was 1st Team All-American, won a Big Ten Championship, National Title, and the Rose Bowl?

ANSWERS GROUP 26

26-1   Howard Warner, Howard's Barber Shop

26-2   Zero, Troy was a kick return player and backup running back

26-3   Head coach Earle Bruce

26-4   Craig Cassady, 9 interceptions, 1975 "Hops" son

26-5   A. J. Hawk #47

26-6   Howard Jones, John Wilce, Francis Schmidt, Woody Hayes and Earle Bruce

26-7   1967

26-8   Jack Nicklaus, all-time golf great.
        Minnesota Game October 28, 2006

26-9   (2) Southern California (USC), Norte Dame (ND)

26-10   RB Keith Byers

26-11   28 point underdog

26-12   Never, this was their first game.

26-13   1963, because of the JFK assassination

26-14   One time, 2006

26-15   IN and OUT Burger

26-16   Antoine Winfield

26-17   (4) Bill Willis, Lou Groza, Dante Lavelli and Paul Warfield, (1) coach Paul Brown

26-18   QB Troy Smith

26-19   Dave Francis, 1962, 31 carries, 186 yards

26-20   Aurealius Thomas

QUESTIONS GROUP 27

27-1   Who was the All-American end in 1958 who also held the school record in discus and shot-put?

27-2   Varsity "O" President Waldo and which Athletic Director started the Athletics Hall of Fame at OSU?

27-3   What was the winning Pick-4 number in Ohio's Lottery November 18, 2006?

27-4   How many players were drafted in the first round of the 2006 NFL draft? Name them.

27-5   What year was Ohio State ranked #1 in football and basketball?

27-6   What two Big Ten schools have won an NCAA National Championship in football, basketball and baseball?

27-7   Who was the MVP for the 2006 Big Ten Champions, Ohio State Buckeyes?

27-8   Who was drafted (1 of 11) in 1976 before two-time Heisman Trophy winner Archie Griffin?

27-9   Who set the Ohio State record for receptions by a running back with 47 catches?

27-10   Who was known as "Wagon?"

27-11   The acronym TSUN stands for what?

27-12   **T or F**   Ohio State plays in front of a million "fans in the stands" annually?

27-13   What two players were on the cover of the 2007 BCS National Championship Game program?

27-14   What years was Jim Tressel an assistant coach at Ohio State under head coach Earle Bruce?

27-15   How many days were there between the 2006 OSU-Michigan game and the BCS Championship game?

27-16   **T or F**   The underdog has won straight up, not just covering the Vegas spread, 6 of the last 8 BCS Championship games through 2006-07 season.

27-17   Who was the second Ohio State QB to BEAT MICHIGAN three times in a row?

27-18   Name the running backs who have put together back-to-back 1,000-yard rushing seasons?

27-19   Who was the Buckeye "Fun Bunch?"

27-20   What National award did sophomore All-American LB James Laurinaitis win in 2006?

ANSWERS GROUP 27

27-1   Jim Marshall

27-2   AD Ed Weaver, first class 1977

27-3   4239. Same as the score OSU 42, Michigan 39 STRANGE!

27-4   5 AJ Hawk, Dante Whitner, Bobby Carpenter, Santonio Holmes, and Nick Mangold

27-5   2006, 11/27/2006

27-6   The Ohio State University and the University of Michigan

27-7   QB Troy Smith #10

27-8   DB Tim Fox

27-9   RB Eddie George 1995

27-10 MLB Jim Stillwagon, two-time All-American

27-11 "That School Up North"

27-12 True

27-13 Troy Smith #10 Ohio State; Chris Leak #12 Florida

27-14 1984-85

27-15 51 days—a long time to sit out!

27-16 True

27-17 QB Troy Smith #10; 2004-05-06

27-18 Archie Griffin (73-74-75), Tim Spencer (81-82), Keith Byers (83-84), Eddie George (94-95), Antonio Pittman (05-06)

27-19 QB Troy Smith, WR Ted Ginn Jr., WR Anthony Gonzalezand, TB Antonio Pittman

27-20 Bronko Nagurski award and he was a finalist for the Butkus Award

QUESTIONS GROUP 28

28-1 Who was the first Buckeye linebacker to earn All-American honors?

28-2 Which Big Ten team has the "White Wave" student body cheering section?

28-3 Who was Ohio State's 7th winner of the Heisman trophy?

28-4 What sports agency called the Ohio State Michigan football game the greatest rivalry in sports?

28-5 Who was signed first and last in the 2002 recruiting class?

28-6 Name the seven years the Ohio State Buckeyes have won National Championships in football.

28-7 Before 2006, when was the last time Ohio State and Michigan met as unbeatens?

28-8 What great Ohio State tradition do most men "tear-up?"

28-9 What is the title of the book about "The life and times of Woody Hayes" by John Lombardo?

28-10 Where did former head coach Earle Bruce coach after being fired by Ohio State?

28-11 From 1914 (Boyd Cherry) to 2005 (A J Hawk) how many 1st team All-Americans have been honored in the "Buckeye Grove?"

28-12 The 1942 National Champs received their rings from whom?

28-13 Troy Smith out-paced the second place finisher in the Heisman trophy by how many points?

28-14 The *Daily Oklahoman* newspaper called Ohio State the number one school for what on July 10, 2006?

28-15 What was the final score of the 2007 BCS National Championship game against Florida?

28-16 Who played for Woody at Miami University (49-50) and later coached at Yale for 32 seasons?

28-17 Name the two All-Americans who played for Bob Stuart at Eastmoor High School in Columbus.

28-18 Who ran the opening 2007 BCS National Championship kick-off back for a touchdown?

28-19 Which deck in Ohio Stadium has the most seats?

28-20 The Wuerffel trophy for exemplary community service with athletic and academic achievement was won by which Buckeye in 2006?

ANSWERS GROUP 28

28-1 Dwight "Ike" Kelly

28-2 Penn State: A "tough" stadium to visit and play in.

28-3 QB Troy Smith #10, 2006

28-4 ESPN-ABC

28-5 Maurice Clarett (first), Troy Smith (last)

28-6 1942 Paul Brown; 1954, 1957, 1961, 1968, 1970 Woody Hayes; 2002 Jim Tressel

28-7 1973

28-8 The "RAMP" entrance of TBDBITL

28-9 *A Fire to Win*

28-10 University of Northern Iowa and Colorado State

28-11 125

28-12 Coach Jim Tressel because he read they had never gotten their rings because of WWII. He awarded them in 2002 along with his National Championship team.

28-13 1662 points

28-14 Running backs

28-15 Florida 41, Ohio State 14

28-16 Coach Carmen Cozza

28-17 Doug Van Horn and Archie Griffin

28-18 WR Ted Ginn Jr.

28-19 30,878 "C" Deck

28-20 Joel Penton

QUESTIONS GROUP 29

29-1 Who was Ohio State's first All-American defensive back?

29-2 Who was Ohio State's first 1000-yard rusher?

29-3 Who kicked a record 54-yard field goal against Illinois in 1975?

29-4 Which Heisman trophy winner scored three touchdowns in his first game at Ohio State?

29-5 Who was the net 1000-yard rusher after freshman Maurice Clarett?

29-6 Which coach taught passionately "that a person succeeds in life through 'outworking' the opposition?"

29-7 Which professional team took two Buckeyes in the 2006 NFL draft?

29-8 Going into "The Game" 2006, what was the series record for the last 50 years?

29-9 Before 2006, had Ohio State and Michigan ever met as #1 vs. #2?

29-10 When was the first year they planted buckeye trees in the "Buckeye Grove?"

29-11 Name the two defensive backs that intercepted passes against Penn State and returned them for touchdowns in 2006.

29-12 Who won the Archie Griffin Award for Outstanding Offensive Player in 2006?

29-13 What state has the most native sons as Heisman trophy winners?

29-14 Who won the Lombardi Award and Outland Trophy in 1996?

29-15 How many unbeaten seasons have been destroyed in the past Ohio State-Michigan games?

29-16 The Ohio State marching band performed what sinking formation at the 2007 BCS game?

29-17 **T or F** The last three games in the University of Phoenix Stadium 06/07 where won by teams wearing blue and orange.

29-18 **T or F** Did the total attendance of NCAA football games in 2006 set a new record?

29-19 **T or F** Super Bowl Chicago Bears head coach Louie Smith coached at Ohio State.

29-20 What was the date when Wayne Woodrow Hayes passed away?

ANSWERS GROUP 29

29-1   Arnold Chonko

29-2   FB Jim Otis, 1969, 1027 yards, 219 carries

29-3   Tom Skladany, 1975

29-4   RB Howard "Hopalong" Cassady #40, vs. Indiana 1952

29-5   RB Antonio Pittman #25, 2005-06

29-6   Head Coach Wayne Woodrow "Woody" Hayes

29-7   New York Jets, Nick Mangold and Anthony Schlegel

29-8   24-24-2

29-9   NO!

29-10   1934

29-11   Malcolm Jenkins 61 yards, Antonio Smith 55 yards

29-12   Ted Ginn Jr.

29-13   The Great State of OHIO

29-14   Orlando Pace

29-15   10

29-16   Titanic

29-17   True: Boise State (Oklahoma), Denver Broncos (Cardinals) and Florida Gators (Ohio State)… all losing teams wearing red.

29-18   True: nearly 48 million fans

29-19   True: 1995 assistant coach to John Cooper

29-20   March 12, 1987

QUESTIONS GROUP 30

30-1 What two football coaches and three Heisman Trophy winners were inducted into the first class of the Varsity "O" Hall of Fame?

30-2 Which player was a two-time All American guard, Team Captain (1946) and played guard on the 1946 Big Ten Basketball Championship team?

30-3 What is Ohio State's worst defeat in the modern era?

30-4 Who was the first quarterback to Beat Michigan three times in a row?

30-5 Which Buckeye was one of the original four to first break the color line in the NFL?

30-6 Who came back with an "extra year" ruling because of WWII to win the Heisman Trophy?

30-7 When was the first year Ohio State was ranked in the Top 10 by a wire service?

30-8 How many points did Alabama score against the Bucks in the first half of the 1977 Sugar Bowl?

30-9 What is the Dunkel?

30-10 **T or F** Mickey Vuchinich kicked a winning field goal 32 ft. and winning extra point of 33 ft., OSU vs. Illinois, to win a National Championship in '33.

30-11 Which Ohio State QB holds the record for single season touchdown passes at 30?

30-12 Who invented the WEED tennis racket?

30-13 **T or F** Jim Parker held Michigan to 8 ft. on four running plays to stop them on the 1-yard line.

30-14 How many yards and which game did QB Troy Smith set career marks for most passing yards?

30-15 Name the three Number 2 ranked teams Ohio State played in 2006.

30-16 **T or F** QB Troy Smith was not the first Big Ten or Ohio State QB to win the Heisman Trophy.

30-17 Who is the Ohio State career leader in punt returns for touchdowns, with 6?

30-18 What do these National Champion football coaches have in common; Carroll (USC), Coker (Miami), Saban (LSU), Holtz (ND) and Tressel (OSU)?

30-19 The Outright Big Ten Football Champion in 2006 was the first since what year?

30-20 Name the five schools where Earle Bruce was a head football coach.

ANSWERS GROUP 30

30-1 Coaches Wes Fesler and Ernie Godfrey, Heisman Trophy winners Horvath, Janowicz, and Cassady

30-2 Warren Amling (1944-46)

30-3 At Penn State 63-14, 1994

30-4 Tippy Dye 1934-35-36

30-5 Bill Willis

30-6 Les Horvath 1944

30-7 1942 #1 National Champs

30-8 35 points

30-9 A major sports index ranking/polling organization since 1929

30-10 True

30-11 QB Troy Smith #10

30-12 Thurlow "Tad" Weed, place kicker on the 1954 National Championship Team

30-13 TRUE! Then Ohio State drove 99 yards to win the 1954 Big Ten Championship

30-14 342 yards vs. Norte Dame 2006 Fiesta Bowl

30-15 Texas (24-7), Michigan (42-39) and Florida (14-41)

30-16 False: He was the first!

30-17 Ted Ginn Jr.

30-18 All five were assistant coaches at Ohio State

30-19 1984

30-20 Tampa, Iowa State, Ohio State, Northern Iowa, and Colorado State

QUESTIONS GROUP 31

31-1   Name the three Buckeyes who have been second in the Heisman Trophy voting.

31-2   What was Troy Smith's winning percentage for the Heisman Trophy?

31-3   Ohio Stadium was built in 1922. What was the first year Wisconsin won in the "Shoe?"

31-4   Which MLB was on the U.S. Olympic boxing team and missed the 1998 season?

31-5   How many 200-yard games did Heisman Trophy winner Eddie George have in 1995?

31-6   Who was the first Buckeye to start in three Rose Bowl games?

31-7   What were "Groomer Boomers?"

31-8   Rex Kern, Art Schlichter, and Troy Smith, all QBs, wear what number?

31-9   **T or F**   The Buckeyes lead the nation in attendance for 14 consecutive years from 1958 to 1971.

31-10 Which fullback was a bodyguard for "Ole Blue Eyes" Frank Sinatra?

31-11 In 2006, which team had greater attendance, Ohio State or Michigan?

31-12 **T or F**   Ohio State was the first Big Ten school to win outright football and men's and women's basketball titles.

31-13 How many years has it been since the first pick in the NFL draft was an Ohio State linebacker?

31-14 Who was the first and only Buckeye QB to throw 4 TD passes in "The Game," with Michigan?

31-15 How many times (up to 2006) has Ohio State been ranked #1 in the pre-season?

31-16 What is Lloyd Carr's record for the last four years in his last two games from 2003-2006?

31-17 Who is the Ohio State Athletic Director that followed Andy Geiger?

31-18 **T or F**   In 1946, Michigan leading 55-0, they kicked a field goal late in the game.

31-19 What was U of M Coach Bo Schembechler's Rose Bowl record after playing against Woody?

31-20 Which Ohio State football trainer is in the OSU Football Hall of Fame?

ANSWERS GROUP 31

31-1   Bob Ferguson (1961) to Ernie Davis; John Hicks (1973) to John Cappelletti and Keith Byers (1984) to Doug Flutie

31-2   86.7%

31-3   1982

31-4   MLB Derek Isaman

31-5   3-plus one for 314 yards against Illinois

31-6   John Hicks

31-7   Big punts by All-American Andy Groom

31-8   #10

31-9   True

31-10   Hubert Bobo

31-11   Michigan 1st (770,183), Penn State 2nd (752,972), and Ohio State 3rd (735,674)

31-12   True

31-13   26 years, 1980 Tom Cousineau; 2006 A J Hawk

31-14   QB Troy Smith #10, 2006

31-15   7 times

31-16   0-2 times 4 years equals 0-8; 4 losses to Ohio State and 4 losses in Bowl Games

31-17   Gene Smith from Arizona State

31-18   True: Woody went for 2 in 1968, winning 50-14

31-19   0-5

31-20   Ernie Biggs (1945-72) inducted in 1980

QUESTIONS GROUP 32

32-1 How many times was Troy Smith sacked by Florida's tackles in the BCS Championship game?

32-2 Which two Ohio State QBs have totaled over 400 yards in a game?

32-3 After beating Michigan 42-39 in 2006, how many games was Ohio State's win streak?

32-4 What was Earle Bruce's bowl game record?

32-5 How many Buckeyes were drafted by the NFL after the 2004 season?

32-6 What was Buckeye QB Craig Krenzel's major at Ohio State?

32-7 What is head coach Jim Tressel's full name?

32-8 Besides playing fullback, Hubert Bobo played what other position?

32-9 The latest "Michigan football team picture" shows nine Wolverines chasing who?

32-10 *Sporting News* magazine named which Buckeye "College Football Player of the Year" in 2006?

32-11 What years did Heisman Trophy winner "Hopalong" Cassady play baseball at Ohio State?

32-12 Which of the "Super Sophs" was the NFL's Rookie of the Year in 1971?

32-13 What three Ohio State assistant coaches are in the College Football Hall of Fame?

32-14 Who said, "This is not a game, this is war."

32-15 Who was the first Buckeye drafted in the NFL in 2007?

32-16 The saying, "Warfield was the Lighting, Ferguson is the Thunder" referred to what?

32-17 After "Spring Ball" 2007, who was the leading candidate to replace Heisman Trophy winner QB Troy Smith?

32-18 **T or F** After the 2007 NFL draft, Ohio State was number one in Number 1 picks for all-time.

32-19 What year did Ohio State change the color scheme for the "Horseshoe" field?

32-20 Who are the two young Buckeye boys on top of Pinnacle Peak, Scottsdale, AZ doing the famous O-H-I-O cheer with their girlfriends in the now famous picture?

ANSWERS GROUP 32

32-1 5 times Derrick Harvey (3), Jarvis Moss (2)
Only 13 times all season

32-2 Art Schlicter (412 yards, Florida State 1981),
Troy Smith (408 yards, Notre Dame 2006)

32-3 19

32-4 12-5

32-5 14

32-6 Molecular Genetics

32-7 James Patrick Tressel

32-8 Punter

32-9 Antonio Pittman on his 56-yard touchdown run in 2006

32-10 QB Troy Smith #10, 2006

32-11 1954-55-56

32-12 FB John Brockington (Green Bay Packers)

32-13 Doyt Perry, Ernie Godfrey and Sid Gillman

32-14 Woody Hayes, about the Michigan rivalry

32-15 Ted Ginn Jr. (Miami Dolphins)

32-16 The 1961 backfield of Bob Ferguson, Paul Warfield, and
Matt Snell

32-17 QB Todd Boeckman

32-18 True! When Anthony Gonzalez was selected the number was 66.

32-19 2007 Scarlet end zones and Block "O" on the fifty yard line

32-20 Jimmy and John McGuire, Columbus, Ohio, Upper Arlington
High School Grads

QUESTIONS GROUP 33

33-1 What was Troy Smith's pass/complication stat in the BCS Championship Game?

33-2 The Buckeyes have set the modern-day NFL draft record at how many players?

33-3 What was QB Troy Smith's career record as a Buckeye starter?

33-4 Who was named the 2006 Big Ten's Offensive Player of the Year?

33-5 What was the official attendance of the 2007 "Spring Ball" game April 21, 2007?

33-6 Which website runs a meter showing "Days since Michigan's Last Victory over Ohio State?"

33-7 Woody would be shocked! Starting in 2007, what can't coaches do between themselves and recruits per NCAA rules?

33-8 Who was the basketball great in 1962 that was the last man cut by the Cleveland Browns?

33-9 What four colors are on a Buckeye helmet?

33-10 **T or F** The sousaphone player in TBDBITL can only dot the "i" once in their career.

33-11 Fred Cornell composed *Carmen Ohio* in 1902 after what occurrence?

33-12 Who is the only Heisman Trophy winner who did not play the previous season?

33-13 LB James Laurinaitis' dad, Joe, was a professional wrestler. His name was "Animal" and he was a member of which tag team?

33-14 Who is the only player to have his number retired that has not won the Heisman Trophy at Ohio State?

33-15 What was Mike Nugent's career field goal kicking percentage?

33-16 Who stated he was going "bald" because of too many 3rd and 1's?

33-17 What was Two-Time All-American, two-way lineman Jim Parker's number?

33-18 What was called "one of the greatest feats in American sports?"

33-19 Who was the Michigan player in 1969 that scored on a 60-yard punt return, and had three interceptions in Michigan's 24-12 victory over Ohio State?

33-20 Who lead Ohio State with interceptions (5 of 21) in 2006?

ANSWERS GROUP 33

33-1 4 for 14, for 35 yards and 1 interception

33-2 14 players, 2004

33-3 25-3

33-4 QB Troy Smith #10

33-5 75,301 WOW!

33-6 www.buckeyextra.com

33-7 Text messages…No electronically transmitted correspondence

33-8 John "Hondo" Havlicek, a basketball question, but one every Ohio State fan should know!

33-9 Silver helmet with red, white, and black center strips. Decorated with Buckeye leaves!

33-10 True! Only once!

33-11 86-0 loss to Michigan

33-12 Les Horvath, 1944

33-13 Road Warriors

33-14 Chic Harley

33-15 .857%

33-16 FB Jim Otis

33-17 62

33-18 Vic Janowicz, 21-yard field goal in the "Snow Bowl" game 1950

33-19 Barry Pierson

33-20 LB James Laurinaitis

QUESTIONS GROUP 34

34-1 What was *SI's* pre-season prediction for the Buckeyes in 2007, after the BCS loss to Florida?

34-2 What four players were taken in the first round of the NFL draft in 1971?

34-3 QB Troy Smith won which national quarterback award in 2006?

34-4 Who are the only father and son combinations to ever win National Football Championships?

34-5 Name the four players who ran on the 1993, 400-relay team to help Ohio State win a Big Ten title.

34-6 Starting in 2007, "The Kick-off" will be from what yard line?

34-7 Carrying one of these in your pocket brings good luck. What is it?

34-8 Who is the only running back to lead the Buckeyes in rushing four times?

34-9 What safety was named the National Defensive Player of the Year during his senior season?

34-10 How many times did Coach Cooper win in Ann Arbor?

34-11 What animal does the "Illibuck" represent?

34-12 How many Buckeyes were drafted in 2007?

34-13 Which Buckeye has won three Super Bowl rings?

34-14 What was the headline on the *Columbus Dispatch* newspaper following the 2006 win over Michigan?

34-15 Coach Tressel believes in 'what play' as the biggest play in football?

34-16 Which WR caught nine passes for 253 yards in a 54-14 win over Pittsburgh in 1995?

34-17 Who lived in the White House the last time (before 2006) the Buckeyes beat a top-five ranked Michigan team?

34-18 **T or F** Coming into the 2006 Ohio State-Michigan game, Michigan was No. 1 in third-down defense, OSU No. 1 in interceptions, with 21.

34-19 In Super Bowl III, which former Buckeye ran for 121 yards and 40 yards receiving to help the Jets upset the Colts?

34-20 In 2006, who was the only undefeated Division 1-A team?

ANSWERS GROUP 34

34-1   #4, Wisconsin #6 and Michigan #7

34-2   Tim Anderson, John Brockington, Leo Hayden, and Jack Tatum

34-3   The Davey O'Brien Foundation

34-4   Head Coaches Lee and Jim Tressel

34-5   Butler By'not'e, Aaron Payne, Chris Sanders, and Robert Smith

34-6   30-yard line. Hopefully to cut back on touch-backs and get more returns

34-7   A Buckeye

34-8   Archie Griffin, 1972-1975

34-9   Jack Tatum 1970

34-10 Zero—never

34-11 A turtle

34-12 8

34-13 Mike Vrabel, with the New England Patriots

34-14 In bold lettering: ONE TO GO!

34-15 The PUNT!

34-16 Terry Glenn

34-17 President Gerald Ford, a Michigan center and MVP

34-18 True

34-19 Matt Snell

34-20 Boise State (13-0)

QUESTIONS GROUP 35

35-1   **T or F**   The greatest track star of all-time, Jesse Owens, played WR for the 1935 Buckeyes.

35-2   True Buckeye fans consider the most irritating college football announcer to be Lee Corso or Brent Musburger?

35-3   What is the largest student organization at The Ohio State University?

35-4   Who was the first Ohio State head coach to receive a Top 10 National ranking?

35-5   Who was the Big Ten Defensive Player of the Year in 1996?

35-6   What is Ohio State's record against SEC teams in Bowl Games?

35-7   What was the per team pay-out for the BCS National Championship Game, Ohio State vs. Florida?

35-8   Which RB had the greater average per carry in 2006, Pittman or Wells?

35-9   What makes Buckeye nuts poisonous to humans, horses, and cattle?

35-10 What high school did QB Troy Smith and WR Ted Ginn Jr. attend?

35-11 In the 2006 Texas game #1 vs. #2, who caused a fumble and had an interception?

35-12 Who holds the single season record for pass receptions and yards?

35-13 Of the 12 leading stats for passing yards per season, which three QBs did it twice?

35-14 What is RB Chris Wells' nickname?

35-15 Who won the 2006 Bill Willis Award as the Bucks Outstanding Defensive Player of the Year?

35-16 Who did Florida beat in the SEC Championship game to get to Glendale, AZ to play in the BCS National Championship game?

35-17 Where and when did Florida head coach Urban Meyer start his coaching career?

35-18 43 of his 49 catches resulted in what for Anthony Gonzalez in 2006?

35-19 When was the last time the Buckeyes scored 80 points plus?

35-20 **T or F**   OSU played in a three time over-time, a two time over-time and a one time over-time game.

ANSWERS GROUP 35

35-1   False: There were no wide receivers in 1935 and Jesse Owens did not play football.

35-2   Brent Musburger

35-3   Block "O", started in 1938

35-4   Francis Schmidt

35-5   CB Shawn Springs

35-6   0-8

35-7 $17 million

35-8   Chris Wells, 5.5 to 5.1 yards per carry

35-9   Tannic acid

35-10 Glenville High School, Cleveland, Ohio

35-11 LB James Laurinaitis

35-12 David Boston, 85 receptions, 1,435 yards, 1998

35-13 Jim Karsatos 85-86, Bobby Hoying 94-95, Troy Smith 05-06

35-14 "Beanie"

35-15 Quinn Pitcock, All-American

35-16 Arkansas 38-28

35-17 Ohio State, Graduate Assistant under Earle Bruce, 1986

35-18 First downs

35-19 83 points against Iowa, 1950

35-20 True: Won 44-38 NCS, Won 31-24 Miami, Loss 33-27 NW

QUESTIONS GROUP 36

36-1   What year did Brutus Buckeye show up in the "Horseshoe?"

36-2   Which RB came off the bench and scored three touchdowns against Indiana in his first game?

36-3   **T or F**   Between 1934 and 2002 (68 years), Ohio State did not play an in-state road trip game.

36-4   Which QB threw for more yards in their senior season, Troy Smith (2006) or Joe Germaine (1998)?

36-5   What was the last game played at Ohio Field in 1921?

36-6   Which QB holds the Buckeye record for rushing touchdowns in a season?

36-7   After the 2006 season, what is the number of straight wins in Buckeye Home Openers?

36-8   Who was the last player to intercept a pass in four consecutive ball games?

36-9   What is the website for the Big Ten Conference?

36-10 How many Big Ten teams went to Bowl Games in the 2006 season?

36-11 What is the name of the new field installed in the "Horseshoe" in 2007?

36-12 How many different ways did Ted Ginn Jr. score a touchdown at Ohio State?

36-13 From what Columbus high school did Ohio State and Minnesota Viking great Jim Marshall graduate?

36-14 In 2007, who was the latest Buckeye to be inducted into the College Football Hall of Fame?

36-15 How many defensive starters did Coach Tressel have to replace in 2006?

36-16 In 2006 Michigan lead the nation in rushing defense at 29.9 yards; how many yards did the Buckeyes rush against them in their 42-39 victory?

36-17 Who was Woody's first All-American quarterback?

36-18 Who lead the 2006 defense with 100 tackles and five interceptions?

36-19 Who was the favorite to take the Youngstown head coaching job when Jim Tressel was chosen in 1986?

36-20 What was Texas' win streak when Ohio State stopped them in 2006?

ANSWERS GROUP 36

36-1 1965

36-2 Howard "Hopalong" Cassady, Heisman Trophy winner, 1955

36-3 True

36-4 Joe Germaine, 3,240 yards vs. Troy Smith 2,507 yards

36-5 Illinois vs. Ohio State. A loss for the Buckeyes.

36-6 Les Horvath 14, 1944, also a running back beside the QB

36-7 28 straight

36-8 LB James Laurinaitis, 2006 Texas, Cincinnati, Penn State, and Iowa

36-9 www.bigten.org

36-10 Seven teams

36-11 FieldTurf

36-12 5 ways: rushing, receiving, throwing, punt and kick-off returns

36-13 Columbus East High School, 1956

36-14 QB Rex Kern

36-15 Nine players, including all of the back seven

36-16 187 yards and threw for four touchdowns

36-17 Rex Kern

36-18 LB James Laurinaitis

36-19 Gerry Faust

36-20 21 games

QUESTIONS GROUP 37

37-1   When does the planting of a buckeye tree in the Buckeye Grove to honor All-Americans occur?

37-2   Vic Janowicz punted how many times and for how many yards in the 1950 "Snow Bowl" game?

37-3   After which game did Coach Hayes state "We're becoming quite a passing team."?

37-4   Have any Ohio State Heisman Trophy winners won a Super Bowl?

37-5   From 1981-1987, which Big Ten team beat the Buckeyes five times?

37-6   How many times did Woody and "Bear" Bryant coach against each other?

37-7   What season did OSU have four straight 40-point games?

37-8   In 2006, how many times did QB Troy Smith win Big Ten Offensive Payer of the Week?

37-9   For most true Buckeye fans, what are the Top 3 most disliked teams?

37-10 Who lead the nation in punt-return average as a freshman (25.6 yards)?

37-11 In which game did James Lauriniatis have his first career interception?

37-12 When Ohio State beat #13 Iowa in 2006, their nation-leading win streak stood at what number?

37-13 In 2006, OSU had their first shutout since 2003. Who was that team?

37-14 Who was the first Ohio State head coach to have two 12-win seasons?

37-15 What was the score of the 2005 Texas game in Columbus?

37-16 When Ohio State first played Michigan in 1897, how many points for a TD, and how many points for the conversion?

37-17 What was Michigan head coach Fielding Yost's nickname?

37-18 What OSU great was the AFL Rookie of the Year in 1964 with the New York Jets?

37-19 What year was the first time the Buckeyes and the Wolverines entered into their game with undefeated teams?

37-20 What year did the Buckeyes tear down the "M CLUB SUPPORTS YOU" banner in Ann Arbor?

ANSWERS GROUP 37

37-1   Just prior to the Spring Ball game.

37-2   Punted 21 times for 685 yards, a 33-yard average

37-3   1968 over SMU 35-14, SMU was 37/69, 417 yards; Ohio State was 8/14, 227 yards

37-4   Not yet, but it will happen some day.

37-5   Wisconsin

37-6   Once, 1977 Sugar Bowl, Alabama won 35-6

37-7   2005, Indiana (41 points), Minnesota (45 points), Illinois (40 points), Northwestern (48 points)

37-8   Five times

37-9   Michigan (M), Notre Dame (ND) and Southern California (USC)

37-10   Ted Ginn Jr.

37-11   Texas 2006, plus two forced fumbles and 13 tackles

37-12   12th

37-13   Minnesota 44-0

37-14   Jim Tressel, 2002, 2006

37-15   25-22

37-16   4 points for a TD; 2 points for a conversion. Final Score: 34-0 Michigan

37-17   "Hurry Up"

37-18   FB Matt Snell

37-19   1970 Ohio State Victory 20-9

37-20   1973, the 10-10 Tie Game

QUESTIONS GROUP 38

38-1 Between 1937 and 1957 how many times did Michigan lose to OSU in Ann Arbor?

38-2 With which team does Ohio State have their longest running continuous series?

38-3 Which Ohio State defensive coordinator in the modern era played tight end for Ohio State?

38-4 Ohio State allowed how many points in the first half against Florida, the most since the 1977 Sugar Bowl loss against Alabama 30 years before?

38-5 T or F In three wins against Michigan QB Troy Smith had over 1,000 yards, seven TD passes and one rushing TD?

38-6 What was the score when #1 Ohio State beat #2 Texas in 2006?

38-7 Who lead the country in kick returns in 2005 as a sophomore?

38-8 T or F Ohio State held opponents to less than 100 yards on punt returns in 2006?

38-9 Who was the first sophomore in the history of football to win the Bronko Nagurski trophy?

38-10 How many times was Jim Tressel National Runner-up at Youngstown State?

38-11 T or F The Ohio State vs. Texas game 9-9-06 was the largest crowd in Texas football history?

38-12 What game was Anthony Gonzalez's career high for catches?

38-13 What is the Ohio State record crowd in the "Horseshoe"?

38-14 Who said "I think he is the best player in college football"?

38-15 The 81 combined points in the 2006 Michigan game was the most since which game?

38-16 Who is the Buckeye leader for punt return yards in a single season?

38-17 What was Ohio States final AP and USA Today ranking in 2005?

38-18 Who was the quickest head coach to get to 50 wins for the Ohio State Buckeyes?

38-19 What was the final score in the 1978 Gator Bowl against the Clemson Tigers?

38-20 Who said "Without winners, there wouldn't even be civilization"?

ANSWERS GROUP 38

38-1 Once in 1957, Buckeyes won 31-14

38-2 Illinois, since 1914

38-3 Fred Pagac

38-4 34 points, final score 41-14

38-5 True: 1,051 total yards

38-6 Ohio State 24, Texas 7

38-7 Ted Ginn Jr.

38-8 TRUE 91 yards

38-9 LB James Laurinaitis 2006

38-10 Twice 1992 and 1999, four times National Champion 1991, 1993, 1994, and 1997

38-11 TRUE 89,422 in attendance. Ohio State 24, Texas 7

38-12 Texas with eight receptions for 142 yards and one touchdown

38-13 105,708 vs. Michigan 2006

38-14 Jim Tressel speaking of QB Troy Smith, 2006

38-15 1902 Michigan victory 86-0

38-16 Neal Colzie, 673 yards, 1979

38-17 #4 10-2, Penn State #3 11-1, Michigan not ranked

38-18 Jim Tressel, only four others have 50+ wins: Wilce, Hayes, Bruce, and Cooper

38-19 17-15; a Buckeye loss

38-20 Head Coach Woody Hayes

QUESTIONS GROUP 39

39-1 What year did the Ohio State Faculty Council vote 28 to 25 to NOT attend the Rose Bowl?

39-2 Which Northern Illinois RB ran for 171 yards against the Buckeyes in their 2006 opener?

39-3 How long was Ted Ginn Jr.'s opening kick-off return in the BCS game against Florida?

39-4 Who kicked the winning field goal in the 1958 Rose Bowl to beat Oregon 10-7?

39-5 Which Buckeye had 260 all-purpose yards against Notre Dame in the 2005 Fiesta Bowl?

39-6 All-American Quinn Pitcock led the 2006 Buckeyes in what category?

39-7 **T or F** The turnover margin was +11 in 2005, and –9 in 2006.

39-8 What number does LB James Lauriniatis wear?

39-9 What color is the visitor's locker room, including toilets and urinals at Iowa?

39-10 After the 1984 outright Big Ten title, how long did it take to win another outright title?

39-11 **T or F** When Michigan Stadium opened in 1927, was it the largest college stadium at that time?

39-12 In Woody's first 18 years, how many times did Michigan win the Big Ten title?

39-13 Because of the No-Repeat rule, who went to the Rose Bowl in 1955 after Ohio State beat Michigan for the Big Ten Championship?

39-14 What year was the first game with Michigan where the winner would be the outright Big Ten Champion?

39-15 In 2000, which players were selected the Co-Captains for the All-Century Team?

39-16 How many times did Archie Griffin score in his four games with Michigan?

39-17 **T or F** In the OSU losses to Texas and Penn State in 2005, OSU had less than 300 yards offense per game.

39-18 Which team was voted "College Football Team of the Decade?"

39-19 What was Michigan's record against OSU through 1927 when they opened Michigan Stadium?

39-20 What was the four-year win-loss record for the senior class of 2006?

ANSWERS GROUP 39

39-1   1961

39-2   Garrett Wolfe, WOW!

39-3   93 yards

39-4   Don Sutherin

39-5   Ted Ginn Jr., 34-10 victory for the Buckeyes

39-6   QB sacks with eight

39-7   False: just the opposite +11 in 2006, –9 in 2005

39-8   33

39-9   Pink!

39-10   2006, 22 years

39-11   True

39-12   One time in 1964

39-13   Michigan State Spartans

39-14   1944, Ohio State 19 Michigan 14. Heisman Trophy winner Les Horvath scoring the winning touchdown.

39-15   Chris Spielman and Jack Tatum, Defense; Archie Griffin and Rex Kern, Offense

39-16   One game, 1972; Ohio State 14, Michigan 11

39-17   True: Texas 255 yards; Penn State 230 yards

39-18   1968 National Champions

39-19   19-3-2

39-20   40-8, four Bowl Games, three BCS Games and two Big Ten Titles

QUESTIONS GROUP 40

40-1 Which Big Ten team has the largest print and internet media following?

40-2 Which linebacker holds the record for the most tackles for a loss in a single season?

40-3 Who was the first head coach to Beat Michigan in 1919?

40-4 Between 1890 (OSU's first season) and 1912, how many head coaches did Ohio State have?

40-5 Which head coach with at least three seasons coaching has the highest winning percentage?

40-6 Through 2006, what is the combined win/loss record vs. Michigan for Coach Bruce, Cooper and Tressel?

40-7 Which head coach left and came back two years later?

40-8 How many players who played for Woody were drafted in the first round of the NFL draft?

40-9 How many seasons has Ohio State had two or more first round NFL draft picks?

40-10 Which season resulted in the highest number of players drafted?

40-11 What was Ohio State's first 10-win season and how many have they had since (including 2006)?

40-12 Has Ohio State ever had a no-win season?

40-13 What are the most ties Ohio State has had in a season?

40-14 For 1-A Division teams, which team has the highest winning percentage in the last 77 years?

40-15 **T or F** Have Ohio State football and basketball teams ever been ranked #1 at the same time?

40-16 Who said upon his hiring as head coach, "I'm not coming here for security; I came here for the opportunity."?

40-17 **T or F** During "The Ten Year War" 1969-1978, OSU always played before 103,000 plus fans in Ann Arbor.

40-18 In "The Ten Year War" was Ohio State ever not ranked?

40-19 What was the "team slogan" for the 2006 Buckeye team?

40-20 What three articles of clothing would Woody destroy in a fit of anger?

ANSWERS GROUP 40

40-1 The Ohio State Buckeyes

40-2 Andy Katzenmoyer

40-3 John Wilce

40-4 11, 5 of which only stayed 1 season

40-5 Jim Tressel thru 2006 .816%

40-6 12-15-1 vs. Woody's record of 16-11-1, both 28 years

40-7 Coach Jack Ryder, 1892-95 returned 1898

40-8 29

40-9 15 seasons

40-10 2004, 14 players

40-11 1954, 16 seasons

40-12 NO! But 2 seasons were 1 win seasons, 1890 & 1897

40-13 3, 1910, 1924, 1932

40-14 Ohio State #1 .74185%, Michigan is third behind Oklahoma .72649%

40-15 True: 2006/07 Both lost National Championship games

40-16 Woody Hayes, 1951

40-17 True: and played in front of 87,000+ in Columbus

40-18 Yes! 1971

40-19 "Just One Agenda"

40-20 Tear and throw his hat, throw his watch, and stomp on his glasses!

MORE TO COME!
Third edition to be published in 2009!

Go Bucks!™ BEAT MICHIGAN®

Ohio State Fight Songs

BUCKEYE BATTLE CRY

In old Ohio there's a team
That's known thru-out the land;
Eleven warriors, brave and bold,
Whose fame will ever stand.
And when the ball goes over,
Our cheers will reach the sky,
Ohio Field will hear again
The Buckeye Battle Cry!
Drive! Drive on down the field,
Men of the scarlet and gray;
Don't let them through that line,
We've got to win this game today,
Come on, Ohio!
Smash through to victory.
We cheer you as you go!
Our honor defend
So we'll fight to the end for O-hi-o

ACROSS THE FIELD

Fight the team across the field,
Show them Ohio's here
Set the earth reverberating with a mighty cheer
Rah! Rah! Rah!
Hit them hard and see how they fall,
Never let that team get the ball,
Hail! Hail! The gang's all here,
So let's win that old conference now.

Ohio State Alma Mater

CARMEN OHIO

Oh! Come let's sing Ohio's praise,
And songs to Alma Mater raise;
While out hearts rebounding thrill,
With joy which death alone can still.
Summer's heat or Winter's cold,
The seasons pass, the years will roll;
Time and change will surely show
How firm thy friendship O-hi-o.
These jolly days of priceless worth,
By far the gladdest days of earth,
Soon will pass and we not know,
How dearly we love O-hi-o.
We should strive to keep the name,
Of fair repute and spotless fame,
So, in college halls we'll grow,
To love the better, O-hi-o.
Tho' age may dim our mem'ry's store,
We'll think of happy days of yore,
True to friend and frank to foe,
As sturdy sons of O-hi-o.
If on seas of care we roll,
'Neath blackened sky, o'er barren shoal,
Tho 'ts of thee bid darkness go,
Dear Alma Mater O-hi-o.

Buckeye Candy

1 stick of butter
1 box powdered sugar
1-1/2 cups peanut butter
1 tsp. vanilla
1 pkg. (12 oz.) chocolate chips
1/2 stick paraffin

Soften butter and mix with sugar, peanut butter and vanilla until a smooth texture develops. Form into bite-size balls (the size of large shooting-type marbles). Let cool in refrigerator.

Melt chocolate and paraffin in a double boiler pan. When chocolate is melted, take a toothpick and stick into peanut ball and dip into the chocolate/paraffin mixture, leaving part of the top uncovered and place on waxed paper. This will take on the appearance of a buckeye. The toothpick hole may be touched up with chocolate.

Refrigerate and enjoy!

Go Bucks!™ **BEAT MICHIGAN**®

MAGOO's Buckeye Biscuits

(12-ounce) can biscuits
3 to 4 cups vegetable oil, for deep frying

Drop biscuits in hot oil for 2 to 3 minutes per side until golden brown. Drain on paper towels.

Serve with MAGOO's Buckeye Butter:
1 bottle of squeeze margarine
3/4 cup of Hershey's Chocolate syrup
1/2 cup of creamy peanut butter
1/2 cup honey, or to taste
1/4 cup brown sugar
1/2 tsp cinnamon

Open squeeze bottle and pour about 1/2 of the margarine in a bowl. Add chocolate syrup, peanut butter, honey, brown sugar and cinnamon. Place in microwave for about 20 seconds or until all ingredients are blended. Pour into a plastic squeeze bottle. Squeeze into hot biscuit with the pointed end of the bottle.

Eat and Yell Go Bucks!

Go Bucks!™ BEAT MICHIGAN®

OHIO
The Heart of It All

State Capital:	Columbus
State Bird:	Cardinal
State Tree:	Ohio Buckeye *(Aesculus glabra)*
State Flower:	Scarlet Carnation
State Wildflower:	White Trillium
State Song:	*Beautiful Ohio*
State Rock Song:	*Hang on Sloopy*
State Flag:	Swallowtail Pennant Design, 1901
State Beverage:	Tomato Juice
State Fossil:	Isotelus
State Gemstone:	Flint
State Groundhog:	"Buckeye Chuck"
State Insect:	Ladybug
State Mammal:	White-tailed Deer
State Reptile:	Black Racer
State Water Borders:	Lake Erie (North), Ohio River (South)
State Area:	40,948 square miles
State Size:	34th
State Population:	7th, 11.5 million +
State Name:	"Goodriver" from Iroquois Indians
State Nickname:	The Buckeye State
State Motto:	With God all things are possible
Statehood:	March 1, 1803, 17th state to enter Union
Highest Elevation:	Campbell Hill, 1,550 ft., 43rd
Lowest Elevation:	Ohio River, 433 ft., 36th
Largest City:	Columbus
Number of Counties:	88
Interstate Mileage:	1,326 miles

Popular Ohio State Football Websites

www.bigten.cstv.com

www.brutusreport.com

www.buckeye50.com

www.buckeyebanter.com

www.buckeyecommentary.com

www.buckeyextra.com

www.buckeyefansonly.com

www.buckeyegrove.com

www.buckeyelegends.com

www.buckeyesports.com

www.buckeyes247.com

www.bucknuts.com

www.coachtressel.com

www.menofthescarletandgray.com

www.ohiostatebuckeyes.com

www.ohiostate.scout.com

www.osumensvo.com

www.tbdbitl.osu.edu

www.theozone.net

Ohio State Football Bibliography

AFCA American Football Coaches Association
Football Coaching Strategies

The Ann Arbor News
Unrivaled Michigan vs. Ohio State

Athlon Sports, Foreword by Eddie George
Game Day Ohio State Football

Bruce, Earle
Buckeye Wisdom: Insight and Inspiration from Coach Earle Bruce
Earle: A Coach's Life

Brondfield, Jerry
Woody Hayes and the 100-Yard War

Buchanan, Andy
Wise Guide Ohio Stadium

Bynum, Mike
Woody Hayes: The Man & His Dynasty (edited by)
Greatest Moments in Big Ten Football History
Road to the National Championship

Cohen, Richard M. et al
The Ohio State Football Scrapbook

The Columbus Dispatch
Unstoppable Buckeyes 2006
The Greatest Moments in the History of Ohio State Football
A Season to Remember: Ohio State's 2002 National Championship

Cromartie, Bill
The Big One: Michigan vs. Ohio State: A Game-by-Game History of America's Greatest Football Rivalry

Emmanuel, Greg
>*The 100-Yard War: Inside the 100-Year-Old Michigan Ohio State Football Rivalry*

Greenberg, Steve
>*Ohio State '68: All the Way to the Top. The Story of Ohio State's Undefeated Run to the Undisputed 1968 National Football Championship.*

>*I Remember Woody: Recollections of the Man They Called Coach Hayes*

Greenberg, Steve and Lanese, Laura
>*Game of My Life Ohio State*

Griffin, Archie (foreword by)
>*The Greatest Moments in Ohio State Football History*

Hansen, Eric
>*For Buckeye Fans Only*

Harper, William H.
>*An Ohio State Man: Coach Esco Sarkkinen Remembers OSU Football*

Hayes, Woody
>*Hot Line to Victory*

>*You Win with People*

>*You Win with People, (Updated with Three New Chapters)*

Hollingsworth, Dave and Waite, Steve
>*Rivalry Saturday*

Homan, Marv & Hornung, Paul
>*Ohio State 100 Years of Football*

Hooley, Bruce
>*Greatest Moments in Ohio State Football History*

Hornung, Paul
Woody Hayes: A Reflection

Hunter, Bob
The Buckeyes: Ohio State Football

Johnson, Dick
Columbus Discovers Football [Ohio State Football]

Kaelin, Eric
Buckeye Glory Days: The Most Memorable Games of Ohio State Football

Levy, William V.
Three Yards and a Cloud of Dust: The Ohio State Football Story

Littleton, Lucy W.
Ohio State Saturdays: A Recipe Guide to Ohio State Buckeye Tailgating

McGuire, Mike
500 Ohio State Football Trivia Q & A
800 Ohio State Football Trivia Q & A

Menzer, Joe
Buckeye Madness: The Glorious, Tumultuous, Behind-the-Scenes Story of Ohio State Football

Ohio State University Dept. of Athletics
Annual Ohio State Football Media Guide

Park, Jack
Ohio State Football...the Great Tradition
Ohio State Football Encyclopedia
The Official Ohio State Football Encyclopedia
Ohio State Football Encyclopedia: National Championship Edition

Sharpe, Wilton
Buckeye Madness: Great Eras in Ohio State Football

Skipton, Todd W.
A Shot at a Rose, to the Bite of a Gator:
The '75-'78 Ohio State Football Saga

Snapp, Steve
12-0 An Insider's Account of Ohio State's 2006
Championship Season

Snook, Jeff
Then Tress said to Troy: The best Ohio State football stories ever told

Snypp, Wilbur
The Buckeyes: A Story of Ohio State Football

Steinberg, Donald
Expanding Your Horizons: Collegiate Football's Greatest Team
(Paul Brown, Ohio State Football)

Tressel, Jim
What It Means To Be A Buckeye

Vare, Robert
Buckeye: A Study of Coach Woody Hayes and the
Ohio State Football Machine

Weigel, J. Timothy
The Buckeyes: Ohio State Football

Purchase the in-print books from any one of the Ohio State Collegiate Team Logo Stores in Columbus, Ohio or a leading bookstore. For out-of-print books, I suggest you shop on the internet at www.bookfinder.com. Good luck and good reading!

800
Ohio State Football
Trivia Q & A

Additional copies available at Ohio State Collegiate Stores, bookstores and gift shops throughout Buckeye Country.

Comments, questions, updates or additional trivia?
Contact the author

Mike McGuire
27081 N. 96th Way
Scottsdale, Arizona 85262-8441

480-563-1468 fax
mmcguire@fastening.com

Go Bucks!™ **BEAT MICHIGAN**®

2007 FOOTBALL SCHEDULE

DATE	OPPONENT	LOCATION
Sat., Sept. 1	Youngstown State (Alumni Band)	Columbus, Ohio
Sat., Sept. 8	Akron (Hall of Fame)	Columbus, Ohio
Sat., Sept. 15	Washington	at Seattle, WA
Sat., Sept. 22	Northwestern	Columbus, Ohio
Sat., Sept. 29	Minnesota	at Minneapolis, MN
Sat., Oct. 6	Purdue	at West Lafayette, IN
Sat., Oct. 13	Kent State	Columbus, Ohio
Sat., Oct. 20	Michigan State (Homecoming)	Columbus, Ohio
Sat., Oct. 27	Penn State	at State College, PA
Sat., Nov. 3	Wisconsin	Columbus, Ohio
Sat., Nov. 10	Illinois	Columbus, Ohio
Sat., Nov. 17	Michigan	at Ann Arbor, MI

2008 FOOTBALL SCHEDULE

DATE	OPPONENT	LOCATION
Sat., Aug. 30	Youngstown State	Columbus, Ohio
Sat., Sept. 6	Ohio University	Columbus, Ohio
Sat., Sept. 13	USC	at Los Angeles, CA
Sat., Sept. 20	Troy University	Columbus, Ohio
Sat., Sept. 27	Minnesota	Columbus, Ohio
Sat., Oct. 4	Wisconsin	at Madison, WI
Sat., Oct. 11	Purdue	Columbus, Ohio
Sat., Oct. 18	Michigan State	at East Lansing, MI
Sat., Oct. 25	Penn State	Columbus, Ohio
Sat., Nov. 8	Northwestern	at Evanston, IL
Sat., Nov. 15	Illinois	at Champaign, IL
Sat., Nov. 22	Michigan	Columbus, Ohio

2009 FOOTBALL SCHEDULE

DATE	OPPONENT	LOCATION
Sat., Sept. 5	**Army**	**Columbus, Ohio**
Sat., Sept. 12	**USC**	**Columbus, Ohio**
Sat., Sept. 19	Toledo	at Cleveland, Ohio
Sat., Sept. 26	**Illinois**	**Columbus, Ohio**
Sat., Oct. 3	Indiana	at Bloomington, IN
Sat., Oct. 10	**Wisconsin**	**Columbus, Ohio**
Sat., Oct. 17	Purdue	at West Lafayette, IN
Sat., Oct. 24	**Minnesota**	**Columbus, Ohio**
Sat., Oct. 31	**New Mexico State**	**Columbus, Ohio**
Sat., Nov. 7	Penn State	at State College, PA
Sat., Nov. 14	**Iowa**	**Columbus, Ohio**
Sat., Nov. 21	Michigan	at Ann Arbor, MI

2010 FOOTBALL SCHEDULE

DATE	OPPONENT	LOCATION
Sat., Sept. 4	**Marshall**	**Columbus, Ohio**
Sat., Sept. 11	**Miami (FL)**	**Columbus, Ohio**
Sat., Sept. 18	Army	at West Point, NY
Sat., Sept. 25	Illinois	at Champaign, IL
Sat., Oct.2	**Indiana**	**Columbus, Ohio**
Sat., Oct. 9	Wisconsin	at Madison, WI
Sat., Oct. 16	**Purdue**	**Columbus, Ohio**
Sat., Oct. 23	Minnesota	at Minneapolis, MN
Sat., Oct. 30	TBA	at TBA
Sat., Nov. 6	**Penn State**	**Columbus, Ohio**
Sat., Nov. 13	Iowa	at Iowa City, IA
Sat., Nov. 20	**Michigan**	**Columbus, Ohio**

AUTOGRAPHS